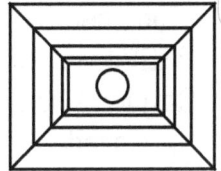

The Letter of The Truth
The Whole Truth, and Nothing but The Truth
So Help me God

With Love and Forgiveness
To All of Humankind
[Unconditionally]

Wilhelm J. Handel, M.A., L.W.

oooooOooooo
"The Spirit of Goodness"
(LIVES)
In Your Heart, Mind,
and
(SOUL)
"Let It Flourish"
oooooOooooo

Published By:
PREVIEWS Inc.
Calgary, Alberta
Canada

© Copyright   54 B.H. M.A., L.W.
               5939 A.M.

PREVIEWS INC.
4209 - 26th Avenue S.E.
Calgary, Alberta T2B 0E1 Canada
Phone: 1-403- 273-9182

All rights Reserved, but all parts of this book may be reproduced, by any means graphic, electronic or mechanical, including photocopying, recording, copying or information storage and retrieval systems, by subsequent, subordinate, and subservient Publishers, with the permission of PREVIEWS INC., Calgary AB. Canada.

Printed by:
SURE Print & Copy Centre
3660 - 60 Avenue S.E., Calgary, Alberta T2C 2C7
Telephone: [403] 235-1616 * Fax: [403] 273-3811

*If you can, Think of and Formulate, a Philosophy
That is Good and Realistic for yourself,
That is Wisdom,
But If you can, Think of and Formulate, a Philosophy
that is Good and Realistic for All of Humankind,
That is Genius."*

*Author Unknown but
Formulated by:*

W.J. [Bill] Handel M.A., L.W.

*Because I feel like I am the Happiest and Luckiest
person ever to Walk on Earth, I am going to
Formulate the Philosophy in Life, that I have come to
know,
Together with some of Its Armour so that Others might,
Touch, Taste,
Take and Enjoy the Fruits of my Labour in continuance.*

*54 B.H. M.A., L.W.
5939 A.M.*

Canadian Cataloguing in Publication Data
Handel, Bill, (W.J.)   01 B.H.
              5939 A.M.

   The compass

Includes index.
ISBN 0-9697487-0-1

   1. God--Attributes. 2. Religion--Philosophy.
I. Title.

BV4510.2.H36   55 B.H.   210C94-900349-2
           5939 A.M

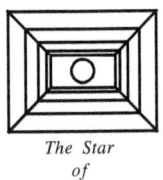

The Star of PREVIEWS

P R E V I E W S
Inc
"Eternal (TRUST) Foundation"

FOUNDED BY: *"THE COMPASS"*
Author: *"SAINT BILL"*
Revealed By: *"The Spirit of Truth"*

The Charity Affiliate: *"Previews Institute of Universal Philosophy" (NON-PROFIT)*

Dear Friends,. This Composition and Interpretation of Life with God, the real, "The Spirit of Goodness" is Super, Super Excellent. It should be "Super Truth" for at least Ten Thousand years., But the "Executor" of this "Eternal (TRUST) Foundation" is hereby authorized to make Adjustments in Terminology Whenever and wherever necessary, after He/She has Meditated on a SUPPOSED discrepancy for a period of Three (3) years.

Then and only Then may an Adjustment be made., and Adjustments will be made to keep up with a Growing, Living God., Yes, God, the Real, "The Spirit of Goodness",. always looking to the Future,. Adjusting Its ways and means to meet and Win any Challenge the Future may bring.

Yes, It is and will be an "Eternal (TRUST) Foundation", away out Front, Looking to the Future, and Newness of Life.

Thank You, as ever in, "The Spirit of Goodness",
B.H., M.A., L.W. "Saint Bill".

Edition No. 1,   54 B.H., M.A., L.W.
              Base 5939 A.M.
Edition No. 9,   60 B.H., M.A., L.W.

THE TRADITION OF "CHANGE FOR THE BETTER "
IS BORN IN
P R E V I E W I S M

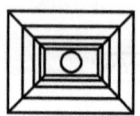

PREVIEWISM
Our World is Beautiful, Yes, Multi-Cultural

FOUNDED BY: "THE COMPASS"
Author: "SAINT BILL"
Revealed By: "The Spirit of Truth"

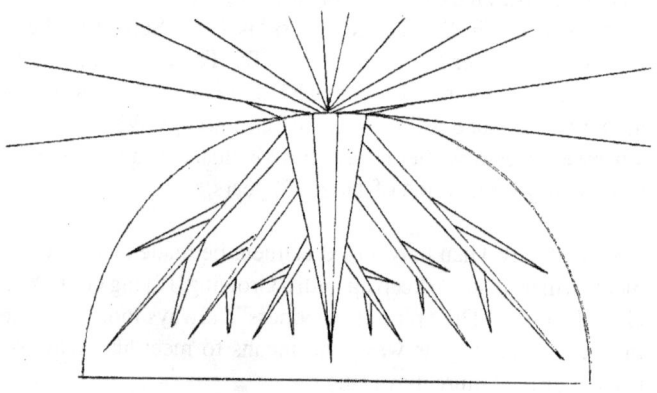

The Tree of Life is Up-Side-Down with the Roots in Heaven above the Clouds. We all Reach up to God's waiting Hand from where ever we are on Earth and we all see life from a different point of View, but as we go along we gradually come to the same conclusion and the same point of View, which is a Broad, point of View, in Heaven.

Yes, Ever Understanding, Loving, Forgiving, and above All Truthful and Forever Real and Alive in "The Spirit of Goodness" which is God.

The Tradition of "Change for the Better" is Born in *"PREVIEWISM"*

www.previews-inc.com
Make 10 - 20 Copies per week and Pass It On. - God will be well Pleased.

CONTENTS

Chapter 1, P.1

Inherent Good Nature of Humans	Ch.1, v.2-6, v.14-15
God's Opposite is The Shadow or An Illusion	Ch.1, v.7, **Ch.2,** P.31 v.1 - 70, ch.10, v.7-14
The Shadow of God has no power	Ch.1, v.8
When we go to touch God	Ch., v.9
God is Reality, Not Fantasy	Ch.1, v.10
When a child is born	Ch.1, v.11
Humankind Chooses Good over Bad	Ch.1, v.13
Shadow can Produce Nothing	Ch.1, v.12, v.8
To confirm the Knowledge of a good nature	Ch.1, v.14-15
God's Basic Characteristics	Ch.1, v.7, v.16, v.26
God will never forsake us	Ch.1, v.17
Direct Communication with God	Ch.1, v.18
Do not Develop Guilt Complexes	Ch.1, v.19
Two Universal Laws of Nature	Ch.1, v.20
Good Multiplies (increases) Bad degenerates (comes to naught)	Ch.1, v.21
Purpose of Humankind	Ch.1, v.22
Riches, Tangible or Intangible is the Consequence of Serving God	Ch.1, v.23
Do Something (Sow) for The Future and It will Come to Be	Ch.1, v.23
Basic Truths and Values	Ch.1, v.24
Know Your Mentor or Your Adversary	Ch.1, v.27-29
God Gathers the Intangible to Formulate the Tangible	Ch.1, v.31-32

God Manifested in Human mind Ch.1, v.33-35, P.1, v.2-6
Confused and Frustrated Shadow Ch.1, v.36
Mirror Reflecting God's Voice Ch.1, v.37-38
Under God's Umbrella Ch.1, v.39-40, Ch.3
Physical Relate to Shadow Ch.1, v.42
Some of the Things Shadow Will Say Ch.1, v.44-48, v.52-55
God Is Future Ch.1, v.49
Chastity .... P.28, 29 - 30

Chapter 3, P.42

Overcoming The Shadow .... Ch 3, v.1-14
God's Umbrella (more described) Ch.3, v.16-17

Chapter 4. P.47

God Does Not Punish, God .... Ch.4, Pt.A & B
Grows Your Blessings, Shadow
Grows Your Punishment
God Set You Free From the
Beginning .... Ch.4, v.22 - 23

Chapter 5 p.51

There is No Bad in God's World,
Only Good and Waste Ch.5, Ch.11, v.19
Heaven is the Reward for All Ch.5, v.14-16

Chapter 6 P.55

God Has No Enemies Ch.6, v.1
Love God Above All Things Ch.6, v.2
When do we embrace our God Ch.6, v.3
You should not fear anything Ch.6, v.4-7

You Should Be Just Like Your God Ch.6, v.8
Show the Shadow Nothing Ch.6, v.9
Instinctive Knowledge of God Ch.6, v.10-11
Nothing Between You and God Ch.6, v.12

Chapter 7 p.57

Good is light, Bad is heavy (preamble)......Ch.7, v.1-5
God takes the line of lease resistance Ch.7, v.6
God's ways and means are very diverse...Ch.7, v.7-13
Importance of Understanding God Ch.7, v.14
God Always Sends Generals to
the Back Row Ch.7, v.15-16
God is never Discredited Ch.7, v.17-19
Act Positively to God's Graces Ch.7, v.19-20
Proof that God and someone cares Ch.7, v.21
Proverb Ch.7, v.22
Remember this Ch.7 v.23

Chapter 8, P.62

Regarding Anger Ch.8, v.1-8
Regarding The Law Ch.8, v.9-20
God Never Judges Against You Ch.8, v.21-26

Chapter 9, P.67

The Melting Pot Ch.9, v.1-16
The Infinite Expanse of God Ch.9, v.13
Regarding Heaven Ch.9, v.17

Chapter 10, P.78

God is the "Spirit of Goodness" Ch10, v.1-2,
Ch.11, v.11-19
Practice Verbal and Mental Tolerance Ch.10, v.6
To Love Ch.10, v.3-5

Chapter 11, P.81
Stages of Humankind's God Ch.11, v.1-10

Chapter 12, P.85
Good Has Roots, Bad Has No Roots Ch.12, v.1-6
Three stages of Good and Bad Ch.12, v.7-14
The activating agents of Good and Bad
.... Ch.12, v.15-18
Results of Acting Bad Unintentionally Ch.12, v.19-23
Results of Doing Bad Intentionally Ch.12, v.24-27
We Really Have Only One Choice Ch.12, v.28

Chapter 13, P.92
A Person Likened to a Container
of Water Ch.13, v.1-12

Chapter 14, P.94
Reaching Your Full Potential Ch.14, v.1-10
Regarding Goals Ch.14, v.11-18
Developing Traits of Character Ch.14, v.18

Chapter 15, P.98
Positions of Prayer Ch.15

Chapter 16, P.101
If You Think You Can Ch.16, v.1-7
Cause of Realistic Positive Thinking Ch.16, v.8a
Cause of Counterfeit Miracles Ch.16, v.8b

Chapter 17, P.103
Proverbs of "Saint Bill" .... Ch.17, pr. 1-7

Chapter 18, P. 123
Closing Remarks Ch.18, v.1-15

Post Script	Page 128-130
The Compass: Suppliment #1	Page 131-146
Proverbs of "Saint BILL" cont'd	Page 147-158
Actions, Speak Louder than, Words	Page 159-165
The Compass: Suppliment #2	Page 166-175
The Book of Insights	Page 176-217
The Book of Furthermores	Page 218-234
Founding Partners	Page 235-267
Chain of Command	Page 268-276
OverLap to The Sermons	Page 277-287

The Sermons of "Saint Bill"
Supplement to "The Compass" See: Volume 2.
"Object, MASTERS DEGREE"
Supplements to "THE COMPASS" See: Volume 3.
The Previewlite Catechism (Last but not Least)

ooooo0ooooo

The Grass withers, The Flowers fade,
Illusions Burst,.
But Truth stands Forever.

ooooo0ooooo

Proverbs 4, vs. (G)
My Summit is My Home & My Home is My Summit
And My Congregation is My Family.

"And so today I hand each and every one of you a Bushel of Mustard Seed. (The COMPASS) As you plant one seed in your Friend's mind, It will grow a Bushel of Mustard Seed. Then He/She will begin to plant. And if each of you will get rid of just Half a Bushel in your life time, we will see "Our Dear God's" Kingdom reign the World over before My 300th birthday." (I challenge you to say, "Let's Do It'.)

The Following is a Preview of what was, what is, and what will be. The Facts, The Truth, the Whole Truth, and Nothing but the Truth, So Help me God.

Chapter 1

1) My Children, and My Friends the World over.

2) In the Beginning there Formulates the Word and the Word is God and God is Good and Good is the Idea and the Idea is Good and Good is God and God is The Spirit of Goodness.

3) Now from that Day Forward God is Active in Us. And from that Day Forward God has been Growing and Increasing in Us, soon coming to include the Words, Love, Forgiveness, Truth, and Reality.

4) And because the Nature of God is Good, Humankind took on the Good Nature of God as it Manifested itself in Humankind.

5) And as God grew (Increased) in us it was Revealed that the Good Nature of God is Everlasting, Irreversible, Unchangeable and Yet Always Increasing and Improving, in Its Capacity and Quality of Goodness.

6) Now from this Day Forward Humankind is Born with the Good Nature of God as it is Inherent in Humankind by the Nature of God.

7) Now Although God is Invisible and Not Physical or Material, God does have a Shadow. And Although God is Real, God's Shadow is Not. God's Shadow, as with any other shadow is just "an Illusion" "a Vacuum" "a Helpless" "Nothing" "Fraud" and only seems to appear on the Surface, But in Fact is "Thought" Below the Surface. And as such, we all come to Know that a Shadow has No Essence (no substance of any value) Never Consummates, Cannot come, up to, out of, or above the Surface, and cannot Overwhelm the Real.

8) The Shadow of God has No power Except to Distract you from Reality or Draw you into Illusionment. But the Illusion is always Exposed and Identified as just that, an Illusion (Nothing) when the Sun goes Down, or when we go to touch It.

9) But when we go to touch God we Find It everywhere, In us, Around us, Under us, and Over us.

10) And so we must Remember "Keep your Eye and

Attention on Reality" because Reality is God and God is Reality. Not Fantasy.

11) And so You see, when a Child is Born he/she is born with a Good Nature (Inherently), But as he/she grows up he/she has Good (Fulfilling) Infuluences, as a Result of the Real (God), and Bad Unfulfilling) Influences, as a result of the Unreal (Shadow), on his/her Character, on Mind (Conscious) and on Mind (Unconscious).

12) As we Know, when God moves the Shadow moves, But God gets the Results, the Shadow gets Nothing; As it is God's Initiative, Not the Shadow's. And Although the Shadow wishes to Lie into the Depths and Insist that it was Its Initiative and Its Result, If we ask the Shadow for Something, Anything, It is Helpless and Produces Nothing, (Except for Unfulfilled, Shattered Dreams) (Frustrated Wishful Thinking).

13) Now Since Humankind has a (Calculating) ability It by Nature continues to choose Good because It can see that Good brings Joy and Satisfaction, and Bad brings Sorrow and Dissatisfaction. This is substantiated by the Fact that there is a Lot more Good in the world than there is Bad.

14) To Confirm the Knowledge that Humankind has a Good Nature (By Nature), We Ask, Who Formulated Humankind, The Shadow, or God. If the Shadow formulated Humankind then it has a Bad Nature, in the likeness of It. But If God Formulated Humankind (and It did) then it has a Good Nature, in the Likeness of God.

15) Therefore, If we were to say that God Formulated Humankind in the Likeness of it, with a Bad Nature (By Nature), it would be pure Ludicrous, Heresy, hypocrisy or just plain .... (Blasphemy).

16) God is synonymous with Good, so to define one is to define the other. The Foremost Characteristics of God are:
1) God is Good (Has a Good Nature).
2) God is Unconditionally Loving.
3) God is Unconditionally Forgiving
4) God is Intangible.
5) God is Not totally Comprehendable.
6) God is a Positive, Formulative, and Productive Force.
7) God is Not Vengeful.
8) God is Not Jealous.
9) God does Not Fear Anything, Therefore God is Not to be Feared, but Loved.
10) God does Not Judge Against us. (Never)
11) God is Unique. Yet is unique to Each of Us.

12) God can only be Tempted to do Good and God will only Tempt us to do Good.

13) God can Not be Defined, Described by/or Related to/or as anything Physical. Not in any Sense. Not One Speck of Physical Form (Characteristic). God is a Spiritual or Mental Image (Form) in Every Sense of any Good Word.

17) Since God, has, does, and will always love us Unconditionally, It has not, does not, and will not ever Forsake us when we fall or in error choose the Bad Path from time to time. God, has, does, and will always Forgive us because Unconditional Love is By Nature Unconditionally Forgiving.

18) Every Human being, has, does, and always will Communicate Directly with God; Because God and Humankind are So Diverse, Each person has a Slightly different Point of View of God, and God has a Slightly Different Point of View of Each of Us in Humankind. Therefore, because it is Known, and generally and universally believed and accepted that God is, Good (has a Good Nature), is Loving (Unconditionally Loves Us), is Forgiving (Unconditionally Forgives Us), and does Not Fear or Become Embarrassed at or from Anything, We can Step Before God at any Time and any Place, and without wasting

time preparing a Sacrifice that God does not want or need, Because we know that God does not keep Records for Vengeance, and is not to be Feared, But approached with Love and with and in Confidence, Knowing that there is Nothing or Nobody that has any Right, Privilege, or Ability to Present your Unique Case any Better than you can. Therefore you may, should, and can approach and Communicate with God Directly at every opportunity, so that you can Forget the Bad things you Do, Quickly, (yes, Forgive yourself quickly because God will already have) and get on with some Good things to Do for Humankind, yourself, and God (Form Good Habits) and accept that you are Free (of everything in every sense).

19) Since we are by nature Good and we receive Unconditional Love from God and Its Unconditional Forgiveness, Humankind need only learn not to develop Guilt complexes and the subsequent Fear of God, by refusing to have any Guilt trips put over It by anyone, anything, or especially oneself; but rather, remember that if you do something Bad it is like starting a little Fire, if left unattended it may destroy a forest, but if you Sprinkle a few words of Apology on it, it will be like pouring a Gallon of water on a tiny flame. It will be wiped out and dead, and without a trace.

(which means you will have been forgiven by the victim and by yourself). Subsequently you remain Free to Receive and Give and Give and Receive God's love and instruction. By the same token, remember that if you do something Good, it is like planting an Olive seed in the ground. With just a few Sprinkles of words of encouragement from time to time, it will be like the rain that nourishes Gods' creation. It will grow and grow, bear Fruit and more seeds for the Planting by the recipient and all who are effected. As such, Humankind can and should simply accept Gods' Unconditional love and learn and exercise the Habit or Process of Forgiving oneself and Others (as God already has) for his/her mistakes. And in this way stay in the Confidence that comes with knowing you are with (like) God and God is with (like) you.

20) In this world it has been Revealed that God has reluctantly approved of, Two, Human "Universal Laws of Nature". First and Foremost, "You Reap What You Sow" and Secondly, "You Formulate or Produce with and from what you have or are Given".

21) Now Remember, God, Good, and the Real, increase (multiply); Shadow, Bad and the Unreal, come to naught. So you will have a much bigger

Crop with the Good than with the Bad. (And needless to say, much more Joyful and Satisfying too). That is Motivation based on Love, Confidence, and Reality. (Not Fear, Hate or Guilt, and Illusion).

22) Since Humankind has Inherited the Nature of God, which is Good, Formulative, Productive, and Ever Improving, we can assume that the Purpose of Humankind is, Firstly, to live in Harmony, and Enjoy the Riches, Joy, Satisfaction, and Peace of Mind that Our God Gives us. Secondly, to Leave this world a Better place than when you came into it.

23) Now if one can not make much effect on the world at large, be not discouraged, but rather strive to improve the "Station of Life" for your family and your descendants, (and there will be many), So you will influence the World a little later. Because Riches and Wealth, (Tangible or Intangible), Joy, Satisfaction, and Peace of Mind, is a consequence of serving God, It is Right and Wise to Build (Formulate) and make progress and multiply the Good and Essential things in life, (tangible and Intangible). This means you do not have to be Poor to be Good. When you are a Builder (Formulator), Producer, or Go-Getter, you get Rewarded. (God Rewards us Well, eh) And so

if there is a Surplus, (and there will be) you may pass some around if you please, (and you will), that is good, but it is only wise and prudent to pass on your rewards in life to your Next Generation in such a way so as to keep them growing. You see, a Snow ball going down a mountain starts small but gets big fast, and then Faster. Just as 2 to the 21st power equals 2,097,152., 2 to the 22nd power equals 4,194,304., 2 to the 32nd power equals 4,294,967,296., and 2 to the 33rd power equals 8,589,934,592., you can see how you will one day have an influence on the World, (In the Tangible, or Intangible Sense). This is also Motivation based on facts and reality, and a little Sprinkle of the Water of Faith. (This is also becoming of God).

24) There are a few TRUTHS and VALUES that have been with us since time began, when God first Manifested Itself in Humankind, and which are complimentary to Our God and Its Nature. They are that a person should,

1) Acknowledge, Respect and Remember, his/her True God of, Good, Love, and Forgiveness, in his/her Prayers of Thanks to God for his/her Health and wellbeing. (Spiritually, Physically, and Mentally) and for the Good things in life that come our way. (Tangible or Intangible).

2) Do not take Offence to anything your

Neighbors Say or Do,. But do Defend Yourself, If Necessary.

3) Take a couple of days off per week. (Things Do improve don't they, it will not be long before we take three (3) days off)

4) Honor your Father and Mother, and Elders. 5) Not kill anyone, Especially not yourself.

6) Honor your Word and make your Word your Bond.

7) Reap from the Produce of your own Seeding.

8) Not spread derogative or untrue information about a person.

9) Love Humankind as God loves you.

10) In the Initiative, Treat others as you would like to be treated, and in the response, Treat others as they treat you, and even more so. That is to say, "If someone treats you Good, you treat them Better" and "If someone treats you Bad, you treat them Worse".

11) Practice the Good, the positive, the constructive and the productive (etc.) things in life, both in the Innerself and Outerself and in the Tangible and Intangible things of the world.

12) Not be tempted into anything that is Bad according to the forgoing or your understanding of what brings Bad. (In other words use Moderation, and your sense of judgement and sense of balance).

13) Gather often to Celebrate and Praise The True God of Good, Love and Forgiveness.

(When you Celebrate or praise, do it in a Circle(s) (Standing, Sitting, etc., does not matter) but in a circle to signify the benevolent Image of God. And to Signify that life is, or can be a benevolent Circle, as opposed to a vicious circus. You know what I mean. Do this from the heart and with enthusiasm and it will cost you nothing. Because what you "sow" you "Reap" manyfold.

14) First and formost, teach your children about these Facts of Life and God, according to the Truth, the Whole Truth, and nothing but the Truth, and God will help you........, So,......Between the Lines.

25) We have hereinbefore described the Characteristics of God that allow us to achieve most readily, the Intangible benefits and Joys of Life. Now we will look at the Characteristics of God that most readily allow us to achieve, in abundance the Tangible things in Life. Just as always, they will be in the Order of Priority. Here we go,
"The Achiever's Habits Program" Part 1.
See Chap. 14 page 94, for: Part 2.

26) 1) Knowledge: comes by,
    a)   Talking to People
           (With two ears and one mouth)
    b)   Reading a book
    c)   The most accurate available,
           ...Personal Experience...
           Knowledge, initially, comes in a

general and broad scope, but since we are all unique we all come to different conclusions when we decide what God has prepared for us to do in life. And when we have decided what we are going to do, we must then begin to gain "Specialized Knowledge" so that we can become Proficient in our chosen field.

2) Planning: Establishing Direction and Goals. Progressively of course as we go along. (Take Time to Meditate) and remember to include your God of Good. And most importantly put your Goals in Writing, so you can keep track and reinforce your motivation.

3) Enthusiasm: This is the Feeling you feel when you feel a feeling that you never felt before. (This is not hard to maintain because every day brings something new).

4) Organization: Order. Establishing priorities. (Daily, weekly, monthly, yearly).
Plan your Work, Then work your Plan until Your Plan Works.

5) Determination: Commitment. Resolve to perform what you ought. Perform without fail what you resolve.

6) Confidence: Faith. A positive attitude. Assuming the result before it is in.

7) Industry: Work habit. Non-procrastination. Keeping busy. Active initiative.

8) Perseverance: Stick-to-it-ive-ness. (Winners never Quit, and Quitters never Win). (Keep in mind of course that a wise person will sometimes go around a rock and not through it).

9) Moderation: Avoid extremes. Eat not to dullness, drink not to elevation. Work hard but not to Exhaustion, Play but not to waste.

10) Happiness: A frame of mind. Being pleased. Contentment. Acceptance of things as they result. A result of accomplishment or successfully serving. A successful Servant.

11) Silence: Think before you speak. This develops the Art of Listening., and reading between the lines. Avoid,

tactfully of course, trifling conversation.

12) Sincerity: Honesty is your best offence and best defence. Use no harmful deceit. Think innocently and justly, and if you speak, speak accordingly.

13 Chastity: (See Page 28 for the extension).
13A Curiosity: Questions: Ask lots of questions and gain the knowledge to Lead the Way.

14) Fair Play: Improve upon the highest sense of fair play. Remember, Life is like a foot race, where everyone is on his/her own and there is to be no tripping one another, because Win or Lose everyone gains the benefit of the exercise. And when you get away out front beware of going too fast or trying anything fancy in celebration; you may trip over your own two feet before the finish line and lose your lead. (During the fall you might even break your leg and have to crawl over the finish line. A bit embarrassing, to say the least,

for someone with so much ability.

15) Tolerance: Tranquility. Calm, peace, also listening to understand or practicing empathy.

16) Charity: Helping the less fortunate. Kindness in judging the faults of others. Forgiveness.

17) Humility and Pride: Be quick to be humble and slow to be proud. But do not sacrifice pride for the sake of humility. Remember, pride is a natural result of Good Works. So if you deserve it, be proud. Just as God is proud of all Its Good Works, in Its formulation, the results of which are all Good producing, so we should be proud of our Good works. God has nothing to be ashamed of or apologize for in Its Good Works and is not humbled by anyone or anything. God is the Supreme undisputed Leader in Active production of "Good" in the world. Therefore, if we can learn to imitate our God and become effective

and efficient producers of "Goods and Services" to our fellow human beings to an above average level, so that we are in fact above the Crowd, then we have earned the right to be proud and God will reward Us. So you see, if you are an inactive, unproductive trifler, then you ought to be humble and/or humiliated. It is also noted that the Active producer does not exercise pride too long on past good works, but rather, flourishes on the present and continual or New Good works. (And of course the further rewards of God).

Notice, I did not say "Future" good works because you see the Wise person knows that you should not be proud of your ideas. You see, with your Ideas you should be humble because they are nothing unless and until they result in something. And of course they are then present good works, of which you may be proud. So you see, you humble and humiliated bunch, get off your........(haunches) and do something. In the meantime us proud one's will endeavor to be a bit more "quietly proud" and also we will endeavor to "Generously Share" our pride as we realize that we usually get a lot of help along the road to our Accomplishments.

18) Be Lucky: Luck comes to those who prepare for, and dare to take advantage of opportunity. Exercise your inherent active initiative. Remember, God is the luckiest being alive, because It is always looking and moving forward to the future and taking advantage of whatever comes Its way and making (formulating) the best It can of it for us. (And remember, there are always a few chips and wastes that fall by the wayside in Its production, and so like God, we must be prepared to do what has to be done, and make the best of it).

27) There are many more Good Characteristics (words of Intangibility) relating to our God of Good that we will share and practice as we go along, but first I want you to know that "In Love" and/or "In War" it is Wise and Good, and always helps,

to know your Mentor and/or your Adversary, and which you are Dealing with at a Time, and then if possible know It Better than It knows Itself.

28) Now we know that it is not possible to know God better than It knows Itself, because It is Out-Front or On-Top and as such is always changing Its Ways and Means to Successfully Meet and Win the Challenge of Anything the Future may bring.

29) But with the Shadow it is Simple. Because the Shadow is a Result, (a chip, a waste, mind you), but non-the-less a Result, Not an Initiative. And so you see, you can anticipate what the Shadow will, do, say, or be, before It does. And you can act appropriately, and you will quickly learn as we go along, that will be to Ignore It or Not to Acknowledge It, because It is "an Illusion", Self-Defeating, and a Waste and Vanity to watch.

oooooOooooo

30) My Children, and My Friends the World over.

31) In the Beginning when God proceeded to (Gather) Bring together the Intangible to Formulate the Tangible "Universe" there were a Few Chips, and Wastes that fell by the Wayside. And when the Light appeared there appeared a Shadow. And God said,

Oh Well, "Nothing is Perfect", "Something is Alive, Active, and Good; And you can not Win or Use it all.

32) And God did not Look Back, Did Not Shift Its Eye, and Did Not even so much as Blink Its Eye, but Just continued on with Its Work, Saying, It had to be done, You can Not be Held Back by the Impotent Threat of Waste, as though it had some power beyond Its Fragrance; and knowing, that Besides the Wind and the Rain, We can make places for waste along the Wayside. And God continued to Acknowledge only that which is Alive, Active, and Good.

33) Then Ultimately, when God Manifested Itself in the Human Mind (Sphere) there also appeared a Shadow. And because God does not Speak out loud, but only by Showing examples, it took some time for Humankind to see where the Action was really coming from, and that the "Sum Total of God" does Not include the Shadow, because the Shadow has Nothing to Add, but only to Try to take Away. And it also took some time for Humankind to decipher "The Voice of God" from the "Echo" off of the Mirror.

34) Now although God is always Out-Front and Above-the-Horizon, and always Looking and

Moving "Forward to the Future: and Never Looks back, We human Beings, In the Following, have to Learn to "Deal With", "Cope With", and "Over Come" the Unfulfilling Influence of the Shadow.

35) Now one of the First things we learn about the Shadow is that It is Helpless, It can Not move unless God moves. Secondly, we learn that It is Dumb, It can Not Speak, or even Attempt to, Until God DOES. And even then it is only a Reflection Off of a very Unsmooth Surface.

36) Now when God Moves and Speaks, It does them Both Simultaneously and very Fast, and in addition God is very Busy. And so the Shadow being a "Little Slow", gets very Confused, and Frustrated, and in "Giving Up" and in one final attempt, It Screams at the Top of Its Voice, I am God, I am God, Please look Down and watch Me; Speak Calmly and Quietly, I can not hear you; So that you can hear Me.......(Comprehend?)

37) Just a Little comprehension, Let me tell you, We must Learn and Remember that the Mirror that God uses to Reflect Its Voice to us is the Surface of the Earth. And we know that the Surface is very Unsmooth.

38) And So instead of a Clear and Direct Instruction

of what is said by The Actions of God, We Receive or Hear a very "Distorted", "Faded", "Weak", "Almost Inaudible", and most importantly we must remember and Never forget, is, that what we Hear is a Reflection and as such the Opposite of what God has said.

39) And so you see what we have to do,
   1) We have to "Look Up to and Above the Horizon"
   2) "Bring in the Decoders"
   3) "Turn Up our Amplifiers" and
   4) "Walk Forward into, in, and Up our Personal, Individual, and Exclusive and Direct "Stem" of and Under God's Umbrella.

40) Now as you proceed in the Stem and Direction of God, under Its Umbrella, you are going to more and more Clearly Hear what God is Saying, because you will Not be looking to the Shadow, You will be looking Up to and Above the Horizon and as such you will Instinctively Receive the "Trust" in God Required to Let your Minds Eye see through the Screen Behind you and Under you, and as a Result you will See the Direct and Complete, (From the Inside Out), Global or Spherical Picture of God's Actions and you will Continue to See, Hear, Smell, Touch, and Taste, to Know most Accurately what God is Saying.

41) And Now after a Short Time you are going to See and Understand what is under the Surface of the Shadow's Fur Blanket. You are going to See what a "Nothing" "Fraud" "Hypocrite" "Luke Warm" But essentially Cold" "Perfect" Being we have under Us; and that It is just "an Illusion" and only Seeming to appear at the Surface; But is in fact at least, but definitely more than Ten Thousand "foot measurements" below the Surface.

42) We will come to know that Although we can Not Relate anything Physical to God (Not one Speck), There are a Number of Things Physical that we can Relate to the Shadow; and there is only One that is Completely Appropriate, and that is, "Earthworm", "Cold, Slimy, Twisting........Earthworm".

43) And So Now Let Us See some of the Things you will Hear the Shadow Say.

44) The Shadow will say, "your God is a Figment of your Imagination" but if you can Imagine me, I am Real". Beware of the Ultimate Liar. The most Sickening, Disgusting, evidence of someone Possessing Incompetence, Hypocrisy, Vanity, Arrogance, Contemptuousness, Brazeness, Rudeness, or being Improperly Developed, Dist-

orted, Warped; Is when someone Says, "Your God is a Figment of your Imagination", Mine is Real". Wow, what an Aethiest Hypocrite. (Obviously and Positively of the Shadow, because there is No-one on this Earth that is an Aethiest.

45) Now as we mentioned before on Page 2.vs.7, the Shadow is Really "Thought" Below the surface, and can not come Up to, Out of, or Above the Surface; It just lays there Flat on the Ground and Says, "Be Humble", and Come Down and Lay here with me So that Everybody can Walk on you Like they Walk on Me; and then It says, "Please, I love you". (Well, what a worm).

46) And then the Shadow Says, "Touch me", "Grasp me", "Dig into me", and I will Prove that I am Something. And I Promise you, if you will stay with me, to Play and Work with Me, for Life; When it is all over I will take you Above the Surface and We will live together in Bliss Forever. (How about that, eh!)

47) And when you begin to Listen you will Hear It say, You are my Friend, You were Conceived in mud, you were born in mud, you will grow up in mud, and you will live in mud, but when you Die, You will be in my Arms and I will take you above the Surface to Live with God Forever.

I guarantee it.
(Can you Fathom that, A guarantee Written on ......
(Grass).

48) And then the Shadow Says, I am Old and Wise, I am Tradition, Do not Disturb me, Do not Question me, Do not Test me, "One way or the Other", Just be STILL, I am afraid you will Unwind the Web I have put around your Balance. (There are no words for what I have to Say about that......, I just step on it, Hard.)

49) I tell you Folks, God is Young and Ageless, Ever-renewing, Everincreasing, Everimproving. God is Future, the Future, and Our Future, and All we Need is a suitable Compass and a Suitable Roadmap.

50) And I tell you Folks, when you have finished Reading this Letter, you will Know you have Found them both.

51) As we go along, you are going to wonder Where and How I come to this Philosophy. Well I tell you Folks, it is as a Result of a very Personal Experience with the Shadow. But I will tell you about that a little later; First let us see a few more things you will Hear the Shadow Say.

52) The Shadow will say, You can not have Good without Bad. (Oh yes, You can my Friends, God is All Good; Shadow is All Bad.) Anything and Everything above the Surface is Good. Anything and Everything below the Surface is Bad, and Anything and "Everything Less One Thing of the surface is Nourishment, or Waiting to be Nourishment. Yes, you see, God has the Ability to Change Waste to Something Good. Everything, Except for One Thing, and that is "Complete Waste", Complete Waste is Nothing, and "Nothing is Perfect" and is just "an Illusion", "Fraud", "Hypocrite", "Helpless", Yes Folks, the Shadow.)

53) And so you see, If and when you Look Up to and above the Horizon, Everything you Receive and Give will be Good or Good producing. Everything. And If you look down or Back, you better Close your Eyes because if you do not, Everything you take or Put away, will become Bad or Waste; Everything, except for the Memory of the Good you Had, and it will quickly Fade. So as I say, Do Not look down, but if you Must, Look "Straight down" and then it will not be long before you Look up......(Comprehend?)

54) Just a little comprehension, Let me tell you, Now the Shadow dares to say, "Turn the other cheekbone, seventy seven times'. Well what a dis-

graceful and obvious instigation or accomplice of Evil. God says, "In the initiative, Treat others as you would like them to treat you", and "In the response, treat others as they treat you, and even more so", That is to say, "If someone treats you good, you treat them better, and if someone treats you Bad, you treat them worse. So the Answer is obvious, "Never strike the First blow", but if someone strikes you in the Initiative, you do not turn the other cheekbone to let Evil continue, but rather, you say, Now it is my turn, and you give him one, not equally as hard, but twice as hard, to stop evil in its tracks. And then you turn the other cheekbone, but only once, and as you turn your cheekbone you warn him that if he strikes you again, you will give him Two back and the next time Four and so on. In this way it is the Evil Initiator's choice, if he wants to be a mashed vegetable, he can, and if you are both of equal ability you will both be mashed vegetables, by the time you get to Seventy Seven. But do not worry about it, "The Good always Recover, and The Bad change their ways". And in addition, (I know you have already guessed), there will be one less "Accomplished Habitual Bully" in the world and one less "Mashed Wimp".

P.S. You will notice that I used the Masculine in the above, that is because we are in a Real world and Ladies do not use their Fists ....

(Comprehend?).

55) Just a Little comprehension, Let me tell you, now for the attempt to make you a useless Imbecile, the Shadow says, Do not Judge. Well, the cold, sticky, ...Earthworm. The Fact is, God says, gather the available facts, weight them and make decisions and judgements at every opportunity and to the best of your ability for the good of your God. And God says, you must not sit idly by and let someone continue in the error of his/her way. No not at all, you must speak your mind and let the truth as you see it, be known. So that the other person can take in your point of view, consider it, and if not immediately, perhaps sometime down the road, make an adjustment to his/her own point of view. In other words, you must make Decisions and Judgements at every opportunity, BUT, only in the same way that God makes Its Decisions and judgements, and that is, they are always in your favor. And to always be in your favor means that when you Let your Opinion be known, you always, as God does, give a person your alternative, which Results in your Decision or Judgement becoming an encouraging Stepping Stone, Not a condemning Stumbling Block.

But the Shadow does not want you to help anyone.

It wants everyone to continue in their old confused way and Suffer, Suffer, Suffer. Yes, Folks the Shadow wants you to be and remain a pointless, aimless, indecisive, impotent imbicile. The fact is, God wants us to Face Reality and call a Spade a Spade. Take what you have, and make the Best of it. And God reminds us every day of this attitude when It says, "You know you are my children: therefore make up your mind and act, Live and Learn and Progress, do not just drift and waste away without being of use to anyone.

Thank you God thank you, for Human Genius and true Insight.

the Extension from Page 14 vs. 13

Chastity:

Purity, Decency, Faithfulness, Simplicity of Style or Taste, Being worthy of Trust. Chastity is usually meant to refer to Sexual Relations. Although God has not Spoken, or even whispered, a word on the subject since its original Instinctive instruction of "Go out and multiply to the extent of which you can afford to provide for, and Play the Game on a "Survival for the Fittest" Winner take all if you can "Basis", it seems that God has approved of Humankinds conscious and deliberate decision to play the game on a "One on One" basis. And so today we should try and/or be determined to stay with One life producing Partner until death do us part. This, seemingly approved by God, game plan has, what seems to be, more desirable advantages for the parents and especially for the children. But it is really a matter of opinion and what you are accustomed to; and it is obvious that the decision was made as a matter of Convenience, Not as a matter of what is Right or Wrong.

We (Society) should not forget this and not be judging according to our standards, but rather, remember that God is still providing Its blessings and benefits to All the Children of the World, according to God's original Plan, which did not provide for discrimination against children, regardless of whether they were conceived in wedlock or out of wedlock, or with the first partner or a subsequent partner. And likewise God does not discriminate against any parents who have not been able to comply to or with their own rules. So what we should learn from this is that, we may sometimes make our own Rules, and claim they are from God, But anyone who says, the penalties for non-compliance to these rules are from God, is of the Shadow, Not of God. Because I can assure you that God, has not, does not, and will not ever, penalize anyone for non-compliance to rules made by Humans. God, we are asked to believe, by the Shadows servants, penalizes at least, for non-compliance to God's rules, but I am hard pressed to give you an example of even that; and I can understand that because God does not punish, God forgives. Yes, you see, God set us Free in every sense from the beginning. So the Fact is, God only stands by and provides or allows that we Reap what we Sow. (That is the Law, Remember) So in conclusion in this regard, If a marriage has problems that will not go away or be resolved, it is the Shadow's wish that you stay together "until death do you part", because it is the Shadow that likes to have you Suffer, Suffer, Suffer, Not God, God never made that Rule and God would say, if you ask It, Go your separate ways Immediately. So if after an appropriate time, be it Seven (7) years, Five (5) years or maybe Ten (10) ......, does not matter, You be the judge according to the circumstances. (You know them best), but if or when you come to feel that you have done your best, and that your Brand of Good Seed does not find nourishment to grow in your partner or that it is being planted in Barren Soil (clay) then I assure you, God has been waiting for you to accept your freedom to do what has to be done, to stop the Waste of you; and to stop the inevitable Crop of Bad from coming to Seed.

Chapter 2

The Shadow is the Opposite of God.

1) God is Good, Shadow is Bad

2) God is Happy, Shadow is Sad

3) God says Stand Up, Shadow says Lay Down

4) God says Look Up, Shadow says Look Down

5) God says Let's Go, Shadow says Procrastinate

6) God says Let's Go and Be lucky, Shadow says Procrastinate and be filled with envy and remorse.

7) God says be Happy, Walk Tall, and walk on no-one, and leave no-one walk on you. Shadow says Come down and lay here with me, so everybody can walk on you like they walk on me, Please I love you.

8) God says Let's Move, Shadow says I can't, I am helpless, I sure am Jealous of you.

9) God Moves, Shadow follows in behind and says, I did it, I did it, I am God, I am God,

Look down and watch me. Really I am Real.

10) God does not hear because Actions speak for themselves, not others.

11) God is Able, Shadow is Helpless.

12) God says Love, Shadow says Fear.

13) God is Rich, Shadow is Poor.

14) God says, Accomplish, Shadow says, Waste.

15) God says, Build, Shadow says, Destroy

16) God says, Be Proud, Shadow says, Be Humiliated.

17) Pride acknowledges Reality, Humility acknowledges Illusion.

18) God is Real, Shadow is Illusion

19) God is Truth, Shadow is Lie

20) God is Reality, Shadow is Fantasy.

21) God gives us our Balance and wants us to walk. Shadow casts a "spell" around it and

wants us to stay Fallen.

22) God says, I am One yet One in All.

23) God is even Brave in the Dark, Shadow is Coward and Disappears.

24) God is real and as such has a Shadow, Shadow is Illusion and as such has no Shadow.

25) God is in light and Light is in God. Shadow is Night and Night is Shadow.

26) God is as in Reality, Reality is as in Truth, Truth is as in Light, Light is as in Knowledge or Wisdom., Knowledge is as in Reality (and all visa-versa)

27) Shadow is as in Illusion, Illusion is as in Lie, Lie is as in Darkness, Darkness is as in Ignorance, Ignorance is as in Illusion. (and all visa-versa)

28) God's Truths provide Ideas, which when acted on produce Good.

29) Shadow's Lies provide Illusions, which when acted on produce Bad.

30) God wants you to be Successful.
The Shadow wants you to be a total Failure.

31) God wants you to be Rich
Shadow wants you to be Poor

32) God wants you to take Initiative
Shadow wants you to Procrastinate

33) God wants you to Live
Shadow wants you to Die

34) God wants you to Rejoice
Shadow wants you to Suffer

35) God says, Blessed are the Rich, Look at them
Shadow says, Blessed are the Poor, but do not look at them.

36) God says, walk around a lake and while you are at it enjoy the scenery.
Shadow says, Do not doubt and you can walk across it.

37) God says, Move the stones off of the field so you can plant some wheat.
Shadow says, Put your head and shoulders to it and try to move mountains, and do nothing else.

38) God says, Man has once to die.
Shadow says, Raise the Dead and let them die Twice or Thrice.

39) God says, I gave you a mate to reproduce with.
Shadow says, Do it yourself, You can, You can.

40) God says, I did not make your body crooked in a day, and I do not make it Straight in a day.
Shadow says, Zap, it is done, But Counterfeit of course.

41) God says, If you throw a 200 pound Rock up into the air, It will come down, and you will realize it.

Shadow says, If you throw a 200 pound rock up into the air, It will keep going up, and disappear into the clouds and never return. You will not realize it, but it is true, Believe me, Please I love you, But do not Try it.

42) God says, Follow the laws of Nature, they are based on Reality and will make you Happy.
Shadow says, Follow Mine, they are Illusion like me, and will make you Sad, Sad, Sad, Hey, will I be Sad.

43) I say, Take your pick.

44) God is Real, Shadow is Illusion.

45) God produces Truth upon Truth upon Truth, Shadow produces, Lie upon Lie upon Lie.

46) God is Reality, Shadow is Fantasy.

47) God says, Money is a Symbol of Goods and Services Rendered and therefore a source of many blessings, Take it Away, take it away, take it away.'

   Shadow says, Money is the Root of all evil, Givme, Givme, Givme, All your money.

48) God says, Love everyone
   Shadow says, Hate your Mother and Father.

49) God says, Excel, do your Best, Today and Everyday and you will be continually strengthened until I call you Home.

   Shadow says, Be Perfect, Today, Finished, Complete, without further room for improvement, and you need not do anything further ever again; and you will deteriorate to a Nothing like me. Hey will I be Pleased.

50) God is Future, the future, our future.

51) God says, Your future depends on you, Do something for it today.

Shadow says, There is no future, Today is the last day, stop everything and prepare for the end.

52) God says, I am Alive, Active and Good; Ever increasing, Ever Improving and always changing my ways and means to meet any challenge the future may bring. Very flexible, so flexible anyone can Please me.

Shadow says, I am perfect, finished, complete, without further room for improvement, finite, resting like a rock, love me, I am Strong and inflexible, so inflexible that no-one can please me.

53) Shadow says, to be perfect is to be Godly. God says, Lets Face it, to be perfect is to be Dead.

54) God says, All my children, Yellow, Red, Black, White and Brown, throughout the world will meet me in Heaven. (the Rich, the poor, the good and the seemingly bad).

Shadow says, Only you who watch me will go to Heaven. Yes, I will take you there personally and introduce you.

55) God says, there are no discriminations, nor pre-requisites for entering Heaven.

Shadow says, Nothing. It thinks It might make it to heaven yet. But It has forgotten that It is a Nothing, a Vacuum, a Helpless useless Illusion. And we all know only Real people go to Heaven.

56) God says, The rules and regulations I have given you to follow, are not meant as pre-requisites to heaven but rather given that you can enjoy a little bit of heaven while you are here on Earth.

And so that you may know how to wear your Tie when you get to heaven. My heaven is a very civilized place, you know. And you wouldn't want to be embarrassed, right, right...Right.

57) God says, When your physical body dies, your spirit does not die but rather comes to Heaven Immediately.

Shadow says, I am sorry, you will have to Wait until I am ready, willing and able to Raise the dead the world over, up out of their graves at once, mind body and spirit. Believe me, Rest easy, I will get started on it Tomorrow.

58) God says, You Reap what you Sow. Shadow says, Beg, Borrow or steal your daily slice of bread.

59) God speaks with Actions and Its basket is full. Shadow speaks with Lies and Its basket is empty.

60) God is busy providing for us.

Shadow stands around and says, Givme, Givme, Givme, Love me, Love me, love me.

61) God says, I am One yet One in All.
Shadow says, Let us make us Two or Three.

62) God says, You must have Schizophrenia; but while Schizophrenics recover, you are a lost cause. you are Schizophrenia, so be Gone, you worm, Out into Outer darkness beyond the reach of light.

63) God says, Live and let Live

Shadow says, Kill and be killed.

64) God says, Here is the way life works,...Test me.

Shadow says, Here is the way life works,...But do not test me.

65) God says, I am a busy spirit and I know you are a busy person, So we will take each other's attention twice a day, in the Evening and in the Morning and occasionally in emergencies during the day.

Shadow says, Sit down, I am lonesome, I want all your attention every minute of every hour of every day. That is total comittment or you will go astray. Yes, You see, I am a Jealous Idiot and I want your total attention or I am afraid you might accomplish something. I have no Ideas of my own, to talk about, just the few I have stolen, and I do not know what they mean because I have not applied them. But I have lots of illusions, so you just stay sitting there and we will "shoot the breeze" all day.

66) Shadow says, If I did not Tell you a Lie, You would be innocent. God says, I tell you the

Truth, You are Innocent, now go you are free.

67) God says, make judgements and decisions daily, based on the facts, and act on them so that you learn right from wrong and reality from illusion.

Shadow says, do not judge, so as to stay an indecisive imbecile all your life and never be able to recognize the source of illusion.

68) Shadow lives in a little Glass House, so the Shadow says, People who live in glass houses should not throw stones.

God says, Throw stones of Truth at every opportunity to smash those Illusions to Hell and gone and expose the slimmy, twisting......earthworm inside.

69) God says, Let's Move.
Shadow says, I can't, why don't you, and I will come along for the Free ride.

70) God says, To Hell with you, You worm, Be gone, Out into outer darkness beyond the reach of light, and stay there, I need you there for reference.

Chapter 3

Overcoming the Shadow (Part A)

1) As we grow up we have instruction based on Reality and Instruction based on Illusion. If we are fortunate enough to have parents that know the difference, we naturally get good instruction based on reality and possibilities and we learn to lead a good and successful life.

2) But if we have parents that are confused we grow up not knowing the difference between reality and illusion and we end up continually taking one step forward and two back.

3) So if you are amongst those that are confused, I say, look up to and above the horizon, and you will see trees, Apples, Oranges, Flowers, Moose, deer, buffalo, and people all around you. You will see sunshine and rainbows. All of this is part of Gods' Creation and proof positive that God is Real and Exists. Now if you look up until your heart is full of Joy and Appreciation you will find that the Shadow has disappeared. The Shadow did sneak around behind you, because the Shadow knows you are now going to ask, what did the Shadow

create, where is the proof that the Shadow is real or exists. And you will find that there is None, because the Shadow is not real and does not exist except as to the essence of a Shadow. And a Shadow is a Nothing, a vacuum of light, a fraud, and as we already know a total illusion.

4) And now you are going to quickly realize that you have the shadow captive.

It is behind you and has lost his spell on you. Now you will instinctively hear God say, Take two steps forward, One to meet me and one to put me all around you. And as God surrounds you, God casts the Shadow away out into outer darkness, beyond the reach of light.

5) Now you may turn around and you will see No Shadow because you are looking up and see only Gods' Goodness, beauty, and mercy.

6) Isn't that wonderful, no more confusion, no more illusion, no more resulting frustration. Only the reality of God all around you.

7) The Devil, The Satan, The Demon, have all been cast out into outer darkness behind you, because their correct name is Shadow.

8) And when you Face God and move toward It the Light of Truth and Reality shines through you and casts the Shadows (Illusions) away. And now you are in Reality. God is with you and you are with God. Pay no more attention to Illusion, because It causes Frustration and Pain, which leads to Retaliation.

Part "B"

9) The Shadow of God says, I am the tree of life, Follow me to the top. And then very quickly says, All roads of life lead away from me.

10) Obviously the Shadow is not only self-centred and insecure, but the Roots of Its knowledge are in the Ground. Well I want to clarify the Facts of Life to you.

11) The Real Tree of Life is Upside-Down with the tip of Its trunk hanging just two steps in front of your Face. So all you have to do is take two steps forward and take hold of the Stem of God's umbrella (God's waiting Hand) and continue your walk with God.

12) And as you go along you will find that as you become stronger you are Free to step over to many scenic side-roads without loosing your Direction because All the Side-Roads Lead to

the Main Road that you are familiar with and which Leads to the Source (Roots) of God on High.

13) I want to tell you what else you will find. As you lift your Head and eyes and walk over to God's Road of Life the Shadows (ILLUSIONS) will disappear.

14) Now as you walk and grow stronger you are going to come to Stamp your Feet. You will stamp them hard to confirm your Victory over the Shadow, and in addition it will shake the weight (chips) off your shoulders. And then you are going to shake your head to free yourself of the Cobwebs. And then as you proceed a little further, you are going to say, God I am Free, God I am Free, I am Free, I am Free. then you are going to hear God say (not out loud of course) but very quietly, That's all right Partner, I told you so.

15) I tell you friends, that is the way it is. And I tell you Folks, It does not matter who you are, what you are, or where you are on Earth today. Just take out your Compass, take a reading, Adjust yourself into the General direction of God, according to the Best of your Judgement, and Proceed. At the end of each

day adjust yourself according to the Compass and take your rest. And from that day forward you are going to find that the Ground is going to get Firmer and Firmer under you, and your mind is going to get Clearer and Clearer above until the day arrives that when the Sun goes down, you will be able to find your way through the Night by the Real and Natural telepathy that God Brings (provides).

Part "C"

16) (Just a little further insight into the Stem of God's Umbrella).
It is narrow at the Bottom and Wide at the Top. And in Reality a Beam of Light that surrounds you and casts the Shadow away and brings you to Reality which is God.

17) When you find yourself within the Stem of God's Umbrella you will find that in the beginning or at the Base it is about Two Arms Length wide, which means that it is wide enough to give you freedom of movement and narrow enough for you to grasp around if you need support. And then as you progress along the path (up the ladder) it gets wider and wider and you become free-er and free-er, stronger and stronger, steadier and steadier until your

Scope is from Horizon to Horizon, to and beyond the outermost reaches of the Earth.

Chapter 4 (Part A)

1) God is Truth, Shadow is Lie.

2) God is Real, Shadow is Illusion.

3) God is good, Shadow is Bad.

4) God is Love and Compassion, Shadow is Fear and Hate.

5) God is Enthusiasm, Shadow is Self-Inflicted Pain.

6) God is Tolerance, Shadow is Self-Pity.

7) God is Forgiveness, Shadow is Revenge.

8) God grows your Blessings, Shadow grows your Punishment.

9) God is All Good, Shadow is All Bad.

10) There is not one speck of Bad in God, and There is not one speck of Good in the Shadow.

11) Shadow says, God punishes you for your mistakes in order to get your attention off of the Real source of Punishment and so that you will Hate God for your misfortunes.

12) The Fact is God punishes No-One. Never. God Forgives.

13) So put the blame and Hate where it belongs with the Shadow for Its Misfortunes and Punishments; and Your Love and thanks to God for Its Blessings.

14) When you realize that doing Good as a result of Acting on truth and reality has its own Built-in Blessings, and Doing Bad as a result of Acting on Lies and Illusion has its own Built-in Punishment, You will soon stop acting on Illusion, to stop punishing yourself. And you will soon be Acting only on Truth and Reality to gain more and more Joy and Blessings from God.

Part "B"

15) God from on High, just loves handing out Blessings. And It indulges to the Fullest extent. And is praised, praised, praised.

16) The Shadow is a Sucker for Punishment; Flat on the ground, wallowing in the mud, helpless, cannot get up, jealous, inferior, a Vacuum, a total nothing, a total fraud, fearful and hateful, and always wanting One for Company.

17) And then says God punishes. The Lying, slimy, twisting......Earthworm.

18) It Punishes Itself, Illusion is the Seed, Lie is the Root, Bad Actions the Tree and Punishment the Fruit.

19) God says, My Seed is Truth, My Root is Reality, Good Actions the Tree, and Blessings the Fruit.

20) It is the Shadow that wants you to Suffer, suffer, suffer, and the Shadow that punishes, punishes, punishes; and wants to destroy, destroy, destroy. But if It can not accomplish the Destruction the Shadow will settle for Waste, waste, waste.

21) God however, wants you to be Happy, happy, happy. So God provides you with Blessings, blessings, blessings; and wants you to Build, Build, Build. But if God cannot accomplish Its purpose in you God Says, Forgiven, for-

given, forgiven. I still have your Soul.

oooooOooooo

22) God says, In the Beginning, I asked you, Do you want to be a Slave or Do you want to be Free. And you said, I want to be Free. So God Set you Free from the beginning. And as such the Law is "You Reap what you Sow".

23) God says, Now, I know we did not count on my Shadow to distract you and draw you into Illusionment to cause you nothing but problems. But although its been a couple days coming, we now have the tools to render the Shadow Non-existent except as to the Essence of a Shadow. And now that you know that the Shadow is a complete Waste and a complete Liar, you will know what to Sow; All Truth and Good and no Lies or Bad.

24) Just a reminder on how to overcome the Shadow, get your chin off your chest, your eyes off the ground and look up to and above the Horizon. Enjoy until your heart is full of joy and appreciation; take two steps forward into the Light and raise your hand to God's waiting hand, and say Thank you Dear God for casting the Shadow away from behind me.

See Page 42 for Elaboration

Chapter 5

1) The Shadow says, If I did not Tell you a Lie, You would be innocent.
God Says, I tell you the Truth, You are Innocent, Now Go, You are Free.

2) In God's Eye there is no Bad in this world. Only Good and some Waste, as a result of the changes in the weather patterns.

3) As we mentioned before, God is always Out Front, facing the weather as it comes. And no matter what comes before It, God always makes the necessary adjustments to overcome or by-pass the Obstacles and carries on in Happiness a Winner.

4) God says, Follow my example, If a Hail storm comes do not say, this is of Good or of Bad. Be Realistic and know it is the weather and make the least of it. Likewise when the sun shines, do not say, this is of Good or of Bad. Be realistic and know it is the weather, and make the most of it.

5) Remember God does not control the

weather, It only controls your Thought, Word, or Deed, through suggesting that you follow God's examples; If a blind person is walking along an unfamiliar Path without its cane, The person quite often makes mistakes in Judgements and Bruises Itself. God then, does not say, You are Bad, No, God says, Here is your Cane, now walk along with ease.

6) Likewise with One that is following an Illusion; if the person stumbles and bumps It's head against your head, God does not say, You are Bad, No, to you God says, it is the weather, make the least of it. To the other God says, Look up and take your candle hanging out of the Sky, just two steps to the right.

7) And so you see, the Bad that is done and the Injury that is sustained as a result, is just waste in God's Eye. God knows that those that do bad are under an Illusion. So God forgives and says Look Up to and above the Horizon and continue without the waste. God knows It still has the Good in you.

8) The Secret to God's Success is to seed only good and It accomplishes this because It recognizes all of Truth and all of Reality and acts Accordingly.

9) Yes, God seeds only Good and does not let any Chips or Waste settle on Its shoulders, and that is why God is always Happy, Always has full food storage bins, and always wears a new outfit, But not all day of course. So remember God says, you Reap what you Sow, and a-plenty.

10) Do a Good Deed everyday and you will soon have many happy returns.

11) Do a Bad Deed everyday and you will soon have to Beg, Borrow or Steal your daily slice of Bread. Because those that know you will not believe you.

12) Act according to Reality and Truth and you will have Rich Rewards, Tangibly and Intangibly.

13) Act according to Illusion and Lies and you will be a Frustrated, Suffering poor punished Imbecile.

14) God looks the situation over and says, That is alright children, I am forgiving and Loving, so you may both come to Heaven.

15) But I do see two distinct differences; Firstly,

I see One enjoyed a little bit of Heaven on Earth. The Other does not recognize what he/she is coming to.

16) Secondly: One will stand Tall, Proud and Happy. The Other will be Face Down, Eyes Up, Humiliated and pouring sweat.

17) You are probably wondering how God can manage to do this with such ease. Well it is because there is not much Bad in the world compared to the amount of Good.

18) In Comparison, Good is a Mountain (Everest) and Bad is a Molehill.

19) As an example, Internationally, God knows there are 5.1 Billion people in the world and only Little Bosnia is at war, at this time. On a National basis, here in Canada there are 27,000,000 people and only 1 in 900 is in Jail.

20) So you see, God knows that the Bad will be greatly outnumbered, firstly, and secondly, God knows, the Lights will always be on.

Chapter 6

1) We all know that the Real god of Good has no Enemies and that the Real God of Good does not fear anyone or anything, least of all Its Shadow.

2) And we also know that we should love our God above all things and animals, but Equally with our Neighbors.

3) So when we learn to love our God, we Embrace It. And then when we embrace our God, we begin to learn Its ways.

4) One of the First things we learn from God is not to Fear anything. And so all the while you are learning to love your God, The Shadow is Screaming Fear God, Fear God, Fear God.

5) Now if or when you obey that voice you will be falling into the arms of the Shadow, and that is what the Shadow wants because it has nothing of Its own.

6) So you remember that God does Not show the Shadow anything, no love, no fear, not even the acknowledgement that It seems to appear.

7) And remember God only loves you, It never

fears you. You see love is an attracting force. Fear is a repelling force.

8) Now because you should be just like your God, nothing more, nothing less, you should only love your god, not repel It.

9) And as for the Shadow, you should neither love it nor fear it. You just pay no attention to it, None at all, because It is empty.

10) The Shadow tries to tell you that you do not know God and in order to learn something about God you have to watch or follow the Shadow (How ridiculous). It is the Shadow that has nothing in common with God, While human beings are born with an Instinctive knowledge of God ever since the day that God manifested Itself in the Human mind.

11) So you just look right through or over the Shadow, (It is a Vacuum) and keep your Eye and attention on God, Far out front, and God will teach you all you need to know by way of Natural Telepathy. (With a little help from the Compass of course, that helps align you more directly with the lines of communication).

oooooOooooo

12) The Shadow also tries to make you believe that it is Standing between you and God and that you have to go through It to get to God. (Hog Wash) You keep your Mind's Eye and Attention on God and when you want to move toward God you walk on and over the expanse toward God. (It is as simple as that). And God will welcome you with an Open Arm.

Chapter 7

Preamble to the Following:

1) Good is light and Its Ways are easy, and the results Joyful and Satisfying.

2) Good always Rises or ascends to the Top (Like Cream that comes to the Top of Milk) Bottom things get Hard, because the Density is very thick and Movement is very Slow.

3) Because Good is at the Top it Practices the Easy Way because of the Lack of Density in Its Surroundings.

4) Bad is heavy and its ways are Hard, and the results not at all satisfying. Bad always goes to the Bottom because it is Heavy, and at the Bottom things get Hard, because the Density is very thick and Movement is very Slow.

5) Humans without Good Direction go to the Bottom.

6) God always takes the line of Least Resistance because it is not concerned with Bad.
In God's Eye all the results of Its actions are Good, and they are, only to a lesser or greater Degree. And the Best It could get, given the circumstances at the time, and Its predetermined position. (The Top or In Front) You See, God is at the Top or out Front and It has to face the Wind and Weather as it comes to It. And So God Producces accordingly and draws the rules accordingly and sometimes there are ships that fall by the wayside (surplus waste), But regard less, we have to accept what is Given us, As Good, and we have to Trust in God's Good Judgement when we interpret.

ooooo0ooooo

The Following:

7) God is very Diverse in Its ways and means. Humankind tends to limit its Diversity of ways and means because of its lack of understanding of God's ways and means.

8) God is very Responsive and Adaptive to change. Humans are slow to change because of their fear of the Unknown.

9) God has no fear of anything, It takes Change in stride or like a grain of sugar. God's ways are always the easy route because It can meet any Challenge, and because God accepts the light and easy way It always stays on Top of the Pile or situation.

10) You might say, God can Roll with the punches and always stay on top and supreme and Unmoved from Its position (Throne).

11) Humans, however, do not always understand the new situations that God brings before them, and the way that seems obvious is contrary ot their understanding. So they decide to do it the Old way only to find that the Old way does not apply to the New situation.

12) But when they see the results of their actions it becomes apparent why the New way works in that Situation.

13) And so as we go along God does not adjust to Humans, but rather, Humans adjust to God.

oooooOooooo

14) So you can see, because God is always making Progress and moving ahead for the Better and Newness of Life, Humans that do not study, understand, or Trust the ways of God, first fall behind and then when they are too far back they begin only to see the Shadow or only hear the Echo. And we all know what that means, Distortion, and Illusionment. And having to learn the hard way.

15) But be not totally discouraged, because although God is always Leading and Pushing ahead, It does slow down or takes a rest when it gets too far ahead. So while god is resting, It begins to get company as the Leaders of humankind begin to approach.

16) And these Leaders then get a Close-up View or Understanding. And while they are talking to God from Close-up, god tells them, that because they are now strong and wise, they are to go to the Farthest back (Behind) and bring up the rear. Because God does not want to lose anyone.

17) And God does not want anyone to miss the True Benefits and Joys of Life. God produced

the Goods and Joys of life for you to use and enjoy, but if you are too Ilusioned by the Shadow to recognize the good that is before you It is a discredit to Humanity and to God.

18) But god, has not been, is not now, and will not ever be Discredited. Because the Truth is The Truth and Real and Its works "Good".

19) And because it has been revealed to you, It is now your responsibility to take advantage of God's Graces, and Your Discredit if you do not.

20) Because God gave you the ability to react Positively to Its Graces, If you do not then that is your problem, isn't it.

21) So do not say that No-One Cares because this writing is evidence that God and someone does.

oooooOooooo

22) There is a saying that says, Wanting and Gaining Wisdom is of God. Being Satisfied with Ignorance is of the Shadow.

23) Remember:

First, You reap what you Sow.

Secondly, You Formulate or produce with and from what you have or are given.

Chapter 8

"Part A"

Re:Anger -

A violent reaction, resulting from distasteful Shock.

1)   Anger is not necessarily unbecoming of or to our God. Anger is simply a distasteful reaction to a distasteful, unfamiliar, unusual or unlike thought, word or action from or to your own.

2)   Anger does not do any harm as long as you do not let the Sun go down on your Wrath.

3)   In other words, if you do not hold any grudges or allow any chips to stay on your shoulders, you do not cause yourself or anyone else any problems.

4)   So if you become angry in the morning you have the longest time to cool off; If you become angry in the afternoon you have **SOME** time to cool off, but if you become angry in

the evening you have the shortest time to cool off. But do not despair, the climate will certainly help make up the difference.

5) So in summary when you have been distastefully surprised you should not allow yourself to linger or dwell on the difference of opinion or method of another, but rather, open your mind and heart so that you may come to understand, but not necessarily unconditionally agree with, your fellow human being. And in this way avoid the unbecoming of and to our God, habit of disassociating yourself with someone you do not agree with.

6) Because if you disassociate with people you do not agree with, you are the loser, not necessarily or unconditionally the other.

7) It is you who is closing your mind and emotion. The other person (people) is quite open because he/she, although also surprised, was pleasantly (calmly) surprised of or with the difference in opinion or action.

8) So the Lesson is, "Beware not of Anger, but of Lingering Anger".

"Part B"

Regarding: The Law

9) As mentioned in Ch. 1 vs. 34, Although God is always Out-Front and Above-the Horizon, and always looking and moving "Forward to the Future: and never looks back, we human beings, in the following, have to learn to "Cope with", "Deal with", and "Overcome" the unfulfilling Infuluence of the Shadow.

10) Therefore the Law, arrived at by Trial and Error, is the line between what is described as Good and what is described as Bad.

11) Good resulting from actions based on Reality and Truth.

12) Bad resulting from actions while under Illusion and Lie.

13) The Law can also be defined as the line between the Does and the Don'ts.

14) Good says Do.
Bad says Don't.

15) God says Do almost Anything, you are a

Winner, like me.

16) Shadow says do not-a-thing, you are a loser (Procrastinator) like me.

17) The Good live by and Above the Law and in Reality.

18) The Bad live by the Under the Law and in Illusion.

19) God stands by and says, I set you Free, so you Reap what you Sow.

20) And to the Many God says, Good Job, Good Job and to the Few God says, Look up, Look up.

" Part C "

21) God "Never" Judges against you; God always says, "Not Guilty".

22) God can be likened to a Parent, Father or Mother, standing 20 feet from a young child just 2 feet from the Stove top. The child is moving toward the stove and reaches up and touches the stove top. The parent sees what is happening but arrives to late to stop what

is happening. Now, God does not say, You are Bad, No., God says, " My poor Innocent Child", here, let us put some Ice or Sauve on your fingers to soothe the pain; Oh luckily, it is not too serious.

23) And God Says, Now I can not heal it in a minute, so you are going to have to suffer some pain until the wound heals by natures course.

24) Then God says, Now I tell you in person, what I tried to tell you from a distance before, Do not Touch stove tops. Rule # 1, You understand.

25) The Child being Older now, says, Yes Pa, or Yes Ma.

26) The same applies to an Adult; when an Adult is about to do something wrong, God sees it coming and Says, Oh, oh,... Here we go again, "My Poor Innocent Child, "Not guilty".

Chapter 9

The Melting Pot

1) There is a saying of old that a very Wise and Prominent man in his town had heard the voice of god, Loud and Clear, and that God had said that in the beginning God created Two Lights, One to rule the Day and One to rule the Night. The man said that his knowledge was Inspired by God. As time went on Many people Acted by the knowledge of this Man, for he was highly regarded. However, Ten thousand years later it was revealed that there is Only One Light and Once Rock. Yes, the Moon is a Solid Rock and only a Reflection, not a light at all. The lesson in this story is that if you hear a Man saying his knowledge is Inspired by God and that he heard God, Loud and Clear, You should take the man to the hospital and have the Doctor give him some medication to slow his over active mental processes (Imagination), because we know that God does not speak out loud.

oooooOoooo

2) There is a saying of old that God once Tempted a man to kill his son to prove how much more

he loved God. Well it is obvious that this man had been confused and this man's God, at the moment at least, was the Shadow itself. The Real God of Good would not suggest (tempt) a Bad and Ridiculous thing like that. But the Shadow did not overwhelm or prevail.

But rather the God of Good (Real) in the form of, or by way of, the Man's common sense (later) told him not to do such a stupid thing. It is said that the Shadow then changed the word to "Tested" because It noticed that "Tempted" contradicted a characteristic of God. But it does not matter, the God of good would not Tempt, Test, Encourage, or Lead anyone to do that.

Now you can understand why it is so important to be Alert and to keep your eye on the Real God of Good and Not the Shadow, because the Shadow is very confusing and misleading as It sometimes sounds and acts very much like the Real God, but is unable to produce the Desired results.

oooooOooooo

3) There are some people in this world who convince a Superbly healthy and normal person that he/she is a cripple. Then they offer the

person a crutch and claim they did him/her a favor. Then to top it off, they then convince the person that it is not wise or good to learn to walk without it.

ooooo Oooooo

4) The Shadow says, you are mine and you are born with a Bad Nature (my nature); Now live up to your self image and receive your punishment.

God says, You are mine and you are born with a Good nature (my nature); Now live up to your self image and receive your Blessings.
And I say, you are born with a Silver Spoon in your mouth, to be Free to choose which one you want as a parent.

ooooo Oooooo

5) There are some that say that if you do not Doubt you can walk on water, and then they say that this is of their God, and if you need any advice just ask It. Well most of us have heard the Prayer, "Dear God, grant me the serenity to accept the things I cannot change, The courage to change the things I can, and the Wisdom to know the Difference". Well,

I certainly would not want to ask this God for the Wisdom to know the difference if this is any indication of Its competence. Obviously, this is of the Shadow, once again trying desperately to gain your A HA.

The lesson in this is that, Unlimited, unrestricted Positive thinking leads to incompetence. And that the Shadow has absolutely no comprehension of Reality.

oooooOooooo

6) There are many References of Old that say that there are people who have been born Perfect or have acquired perfection during life. Well, this is vanity because to be perfect is to be finite or dead. And God is not finite or dead. And so anyone who worships a "perfect person",. born or acquired, is worshipping a Shadow. So just remember that even the "supposed perfect" in our history have said that we shall do even greater and better things than they.

oooooOooooo

7) Well, the Philosophy of the Real and True Good Natured God within us Offers us a

compass which points to God's waiting hand, described as the "Stem of God's Umbrella" that leads to the Source (Roots) of God on High, for you to grasp and follow. And as you come closer to God, It encourages you to then learn to Fly like the birds. (And when we are able to "Fly like the Birds" it means we have become able to Think and Act Freely. Free of all Illusion, Doubt, Fear or Guilt. Free to Think and Act confidently according to the Clear and Real Will of our God on High, which is Good.)

oooooOooooo

8) There are some that say, that if you think something Bad, it is as Bad as if you already did it. Well, that is ridiculous, and obviously of the Shadow, because it reduces us to vegetables. In other words they are saying that we do not have the Right to be Free to choose right from wrong. Well, we know God set us Free in the beginning and gave us the right to choose the Good path or the Bad path. So that means that as our mind wanders and explores, (and it needs to wander and explore to progress) it may come up with Bad or Good ideas. But humankind has a sense, or ability, of Judgement (calculating) and can put a stop

to Bad thoughts and pursue the Good thoughts (Act on the Good) (Not the Bad). That is being Free and True to your Good nature. Otherwise you would stop thinking.

oooooOooooo

9) We thank God for the Good that comes our way, Never the Bad. Blaming God for the Bad is Ludicrous. Some things are as a result of following God, Some things are as a result of following the Shadow, and Some things are as a result of the weather and so we have to make the necessary adjustments and carry on.

oooooOooooo

Re: Doomsdayers:

10) The Real God of Good is not a Doomsdayer. Does not even cross Its mind. Anyone who says that the World is coming to an end does not have much confidence in God's purpose, plan or abilities. And he/she does not really know God. They are forgetting that God is Everincreasing and Everimproving upon Its works. These people are suggesting that God does not have a better plan than one that comes to an end. This is insulting to God's planning,

God's abilities and Its intelligence. So in fact these people are Hypocrites, Saying out of one side of their mouth that they believe in an Everlasting God and from the other side, saying that the World is coming to an End, or that God is going to Die. What a negative defeatist attitude. Obviously of the Shadow. Anyone who believes in the Eternity of God will realize that God will adjust to whatever comes Its way and survive Eternally.

oooooOooooo

11) Should someone ever say to you, I did a certain Something for you because I love you, Now you Owe me.

You just say, be gone you worm (Shadow), You do not know what love is. Yes, you illegit, to love is to give without expecting a return. So I do not care if you would die for me, if you did it out of love, I would owe you nothing. So be gone you cold slimmy twisting......Earthworm.

oooooOooooo

12) You might be interested to know that the Shadow is the only thing that "Seems to

Appear" in God's Formulation that Qualifies to have an Inferiority Complex. Yes, everything in God's total world (Universe) is something and has some value. But the Shadow is, a Nothing, a Vacuum, an Illusion, and at the most an Earthworm seeming to appear on the surface. And so you can see why this supposed character goes to such disgusting, filthy Extremes to try to be somebody. As a matter of fact, One of these days It (the Shadow) might even suggest to you that It will offer Itself to God as a Ransom for your Unfounded Guilt toward God. Yes, the Guilt the Shadow Itself will attempt to lead you to believe exists. Well, I want to tell you that if this should ever be proposed to you, you just remember that what the Twisting worm is trying to do is to get the advantage on God, and use You as a Ransom for Itself. But do not worry, God will not Hear of it.

Because God knows the Truth, and is always Loving and Forgiving towards Its own children. For God knows you have already paid the Penalty for your Wrong Doings with the Built-in Punishment that you Suffered while on Earth. So when God judges you the Verdict is always "Not Guilty" and God says, Come-on into My Home (Heaven), no Admission necessary, You are my Children in the Beginning and you are My Children Now and unto Eternity, Welcome Home.

ooooooOoooooo

13) The Infinite expanse of God.
God is not limited to any one person's knowledge of it. But rather, God is so diverse that It reveals Itself as Unique to each of us on Earth. And so the Compass is a general overall Underview of God, but if we took the interpretations of every Human being in the World and put them all together we would have an Underall Overview of God on High to the Extent of Its present stage of Its Manifestation in the Human Sphere.

ooooooOoooooo

14) There are some people in this world that say that Faith without works is Dead, out of one side of their mouth and out of the other side they say that one is saved by Faith alone. Well, if this is not Outright hypocrisy then it certainly is sitting on the Fence; not knowing who you are, what you are, where you are going, or where you came from. Confused. Obviously of the Shadow.

15) The Real God of Good comes straight out and says All of Humankind is allowed into God's Circle of friends around the Universe of Universes (Heaven), unconditionally. But if you want a little bit of Heaven while you are here on Earth you better do some Good Works.

oooooOooooo

16) Only Human beings are allowed into Heaven, Not Gods. God does not need anymore Gods around. The Shadow leads you to believe you are Gods, and that you must be Gods to enter Heaven. (Hog Wash). God accepts you into Heaven, for who you are, what you are and As you are, out of Love and Mercy. And you do not have to do anything for God for the Acceptance. You just have to do something for others here on Earth. (Remember God set you Free and therefore "You Reap what you Sow" on Earth.) But when it is time for Heaven you are Accepted by God's Grace. There is no Ransom to pay and no Sacrifice to make. God Forgives you, as It already has, and Accepts you by mercy and grace.

17) **Re: Heaven**

First of All let us talk about your Spirit (Soul). Your Spirit can be described as a Little Bubble (Clean as a Whistle) and is Lighter than Air and Lighter than Light. And so it floats Up, Over and Away Out to Outer Space to the End of a Light Ray; and there it sits with its back to outer darkness and its face to inner light. And of course there is Lots of Company, so everyone holds hands in a Big Big Circle around our Magnificent God. Of course there is always Room for more because it is an expanding Sphere or Globe with the Universe inside and the Sun in the Centre. And so we sit and Giggle, chat and sing praises to our dear God and watch the World go by. (How about that eh.)

God is really Imaginative and Creative, isn't It, eh; not like the Shadow, which in this regard, could only think about where It's next slice of bread was coming from.

Chapter 10

God is Good Spirit and Good Spirit is God

1) God is Good and Good is, Sincerity, Love, Forgiveness, Knowledge, Planning, Enthusiasm, Organization, Determination, Confidence, Industry, Perseverance, Moderation, Happiness, Silence, Appreciation, Chastity, Fair Play, Tolerance, Charity, (Pride and Humility), Being Lucky, and Feeling as Unique in God as God is Unique in You.

2) All of the above Qualities of God form a chain; and we all know that a chain is only as strong as its weakest Link.

    Therefore, to say that one quality is everything, without it you have nothing, is of the Shadow.

    Yes, the reality of this chain is that each link strengthens the other and the total becomes very strong. But if you hold one by itself, it becomes very weak and shallow like fool's gold.

oooooOooooo

3) To love is to give without expecting a return. God's love is love that gives without expecting a return.

4) Humans can love without expecting a return only while their reserve of love is well above empty. And in order to keep their reserve of love full or near full, they need to practice accepting and appreciating God's love and Goodness that comes their way everyday. By appreciating, accepting and thanking God for our "Good Fortune" every day, we build our ability to love or give of our love, without expecting a return.

5) If we do not draw on God's love, our love becomes a "need", not love at all, because it becomes, I give but I need, want or demand a return. This is setting the footing to slavery not freedom. So you see God's love is free and it leaves you free; so accept God's love and pass it on and it will grow and grow.

oooooOooooo

6) Practice and develop more and more verbal or mental tolerance and understanding so that you do not strike the first (physical) blow. This is becoming of and to our God.

3) To love is to give without expecting a return. God's love is love that gives without expecting a return.

4) Humans can love without expecting a return only while their reserve of love is well above empty. And in order to keep their reserve of love full or near full, they need to practice accepting and appreciating God's love and Goodness that comes their way everyday. By appreciating, accepting and thanking God for our "Good Fortune" every day, we build our ability to love or give of our love, without expecting a return.

5) If we do not draw on God's love, our love becomes a "need", not love at all, because it becomes, I give but I need, want or demand a return. This is setting the footing to slavery not freedom. So you see God's love is free and it leaves you free; so accept God's love and pass it on and it will grow and grow.

oooooOooooo

6) Practice and develop more and more verbal or mental tolerance and understanding so that you do not strike the first (physical) blow. This is becoming of and to our God.

oooooOooooo

7) God says, Always be a bit more proud than humble. Shadow says, be completely humble and have no pride at all.

8) God says, Help the poor out of their misery, not in their misery.

   Shadow says, Join us and become one of us, with your barrel of wine, and let us drink and forget our poverty and remember our misery no more.

9) God says, Be Generous.
   Shadow says, Be Shamelessly Greedy.

10) God says, Give some to Charity.
    Shadow says, Give your All to me; your last One Hundred Thousand Dollars, or your last three pennies; either way I will take it.

11) God says, Judge and be Judged, in God's fashion, to keep you straight and let you grow in Reality and Truth.

    Shadow says, Do not Judge, or else you may be Judged, to keep you crooked and let you continue in Illusion and Lie.

12) God says, Do not condemn anyone.
Shadow says, you are all condemned.

13) God says, from the sky you come and to the sky you go.
Shadow says, from Dirt you came, to dirt you go.

14) I say, TAKE your pick, I did, and I am Happy go Lucky with it.

Chapter 11

"Part A"

1) God was, is and always shall be Good and Good producing and improving It's lot. And regardless of what Mutations It has as It goes along the results are always Good and better as God is a progressive, inherently excellence seeking God.

2) Stages of Humankind's God.

3) 50,000 years ago, Primitive Man's God: (Physical or Tangible) Mostly live animals probably because Humans had not yet learned to talk, and the animals were probably smarter than the Humans.

4) 20,000 years ago, Cave Man's God:
Humans had begun to draw pictures so the Image of God took shape in Dead Animals.

5) 10,000 years ago, Ancient Man's God:
Humans began to develop a language (Vocabulary). So the Image of God gradually took shape in popular Humans.

6) 6,000 years ago, Semi-Civilized Man's God:
Language had developed sufficiently for the Image of God to take on an Intangible form. But not clearly defined whether it had a Good Nature or a Bad Nature.

7) 50 years ago, Civilized Man's God:
The Seeds were planted for the Real Intangible, Good Natured, Loving, Forgiving, Positive, Formulative, Productive, Everincreasing, Everimproving, Everlasting, "Pure Good Producing", God to Emerge. Based on Truth and Reality not Illusion and Lie.

8) 1 year ago, Civilized Man's God :
A "Good Natured God" with all the inherent co-incidental qualities of Good, Emerged in the Neuter Gender.

9) Present: Civilized Human Beings' God:

Although the Original Blueprints were lost the Eternal Living "Real God of Good" has been recognized and identified from the results of Its actions not the lies of Its Shadow.

But at any rate because of the long lapse of time and distance it is realized that God will never be totally comprehendible, even in the Neuter Gender. Sorry Ladies, but that is the way the ball bounces, eh. You cannot win them all, eh. Ho, Ho, Ho.

"Part "B"

10) God is "The Spirit of Goodness" and has many characteristics.

11) God manifests Itself in a selection of words (Ideas) arranged such that they form a psyche (psychology) based on reality which bears a good product (Fruit), that is agreeable and acceptable to all of Humankind.

12) A psychology that brings out a Happy disposition.

13) A psychology that brings out a Lucky disposition.

14) A psychology that brings out a Sincere disposition.

15) A psychology that brings out a Loving disposition.

16) A psychology that brings out a Confident disposition.

17) A psychology that brings out All of the Good Characteristics of God that we know herein including a sense of Judgement and a sense of Balance.

18) And finally, a psychology that leaves us free of all Illusion, doubt, fear, or guilt. And one that brings us to reality which is God, being free of any physically or mentally impairing forces.

oooooOooooo

19) God and Its Good does not recognize or acknowledge Its Shadow and Its unfulfilling Bad influence. God only recognizes different degrees or levels of Good. And rather than use the inappropriate word "Bad", God says you are either rich in good or poor in Good, but always Good. So you see all of (and from) God is Good in the tangible or intangible

forms, from the level of one degree up to 100 and on up to infinity degrees. Yes, All have a purpose in the Balance of Nature.

Chapter 12

1) The Good of God and inherently the Good of Humankind has roots.

2) The Bad of Humankind, which is as a result of watching the Shadow, has no roots.

3) The Good of Humankind is like the Grass, it starts out below the Surface, grows roots, then grows some more to mature, bear fruit and more seed. (It has Roots).

4) But the Bad of Humankind is like a Fire. It starts above or near the surface, it comes in with a bang but immediately begins to die. Although it may Singe the grass it cannot get past the surface and so it goes out and dies.

5) Subsequently the Good, having Roots, regenerates, replenishes and again bears Fruit.

6) This is why God does not worry about the Shadow. Because God is a multiplying,

growing and living force. The Shadow is a degenerating, dying and no real lasting force.

On the subject of the Innerself.

7) Good and Bad, by their own merits, both can and do exist, in the Static form. Good when Activated, regenerates, grows roots, bears fruit and ultimately more Seed.

8) But Bad when activated, degenerates, grows No roots, but rather consumes itself, dies and leaves only ashes.

9) Therefore Good and Bad basically have three forms.

10) For the Good they are:
1) Static
2) Active Regenerating and
3) Living

11) For the Bad they are:
1) Static
2) Active Degenerating and
3) Dead.

12) The Good is Activated by an Act of Love (word or deed), is kept actively regenerating by the water of encouragement and comes to

maturity or life basically on Its own, as long as there are no unforeseen natural or unnatural disasters.

13) The Bad is Activated by an Act of Hate (word or deed), then it is on Fire and Actively Degenerating. If there is nothing in Its path it burns out and dies without a trace. If there is something in its path, if left unattended it will and can only consume down to the surface and forward to the river, then it dies and leaves only ashes. (which are soon washed away by the water of life (Tangible or intangible.)

14) Naturally in life when there is a Fire (of the Bad) the Good will attempt to pour water on it to put it out. But if it is too Hot or Fierce, then you just sprinkle the outer edges to keep it from spreading. Then naturally it will burn itself out and die. In this case it will usually leave a Scar, but the Scar will heal and be forgotten.

15) I go back a step to clearly identify the activating agents of the static forms of Good and Bad. I said that an Act of Love is the Agent for activating Good Static.

16) Well the Act is by physical word or deed, not

just the thought of it.

17) The Thought by itself is not the agent, the thought alone, in fact is the storing or building up of the Static Form, and is released or activated by your own or someone else's Act of Love by word or deed.

18) The same process applies to the Bad Static, if you allow yourself to dwell on Bad thoughts you are storing up the Bad Static form. The greater the level of Static in either form (Good or Bad) the greater the chance of it being activated by your own or someone else's corresponding Act by word or deed of either Love or Hate.

19) Let us go back a few steps again and talk about the freedom of thought and motion that is inherent in us when we enter this world. As we mentioned before God brings us into this world in the free form. This means free of physical vices and free of mental guilt. (Free of Physically or Mentally impairing forces).

20) When we are young and growing up our parents and elders teach us what they think is positive, creative and productive in life and what is Good for you and others in life and finally

what brings riches, joy, satisfaction and peace of mind.

21) As we mature we begin to apply the teaching and knowledge in our daily lives in making decisions of our own with regard to our New and personal circumstances.

22) Because our mind is free to wander, explore and calculate, it comes up with some Good and some Bad ideas. And because of our nature we tend to and want to act on the good ideas for maximum and best results. Sometimes we unintentionally act on a Bad idea (Illusion) not recognizing its true nature until we get Bad results and Bad Effects for ourselves as well as others. These kind of Bad actions do not do any serious or lasting damage to our character or mental efficiency or freedom.

23) But rather, they become stepping stones to a better sense of judgement.

24) However, if we intentionally act on a Bad Idea, knowing it is Bad, it starts a little fire in our Innerself, (because it is against our natural Good Instincts) and destroys a little of the good fibre in us, like our self-respect, our

confidence to be able to make Good decisions and other characteristics of this Nature. (This translates into impairments to our freedom of thought in the Innerself) On the outerself you are laying the foundation for a Bad Reputation and for Bad Fruits to come your way.

25) So you see these kinds of actions become stumbling blocks in our lives. If we do these bad actions intentionally and awarely, but only occasionally, we can regain and rebuild the positives we had. But no matter how you look at it, it is a waste of time and effort to take a step or two backward in the Innerself for the sake of a physical or tangible gain. (A physical or tangible gain, no matter how big, is never worth the loss of an Inner Good Quality (Fibre), no matter how small).

26) Ultimately I want you to know that, if you continually, consciously and intentionally do Bad actions or words, You are a Sucker for Punishment like the Shadow and your Bad Habits will become stronger and stronger until they are like chains around you. Yes, you will lead yourself to Bondage, Suffering and Punishment.

27) As your Bad Habits become stronger your character becomes weaker until One day you will have to ask someone to Lift your chin off your Chest, put Tooth Picks between your eye lids and take you two steps to the right.

28) And so you see, there is really only One choice in this world and that is to Foster and Seed the Inherent Good of God that is in you, so that you might enjoy and receive a little of heaven right here on Earth and ultimately stand tall, proud and happy in God's Eternal Heaven. (As opposed to Bearing unnecessary suffering and punishment all your life and then having to Stand Face Down, Eyes up, humiliated and pouring sweat before God.)

29) I mean, think about it, and then tell me with a straight face that you think there are two choices. (I know, you have already guessed, you cannot do it Unless you Lie, and you need not lie before God.)

oooooOooooo

Chapter 13

1) A person can be likened to a container of water; if you add a "Good" cube of sugar and spice it dissolves and enriches the water, but if you add a "Bad" rock, it goes to the bottom and effects nothing.

2) Now when the water evaporates the sugar is again found at the bottom along with the Rock. The sugar is taken and used time and time again. The Rock is left behind because it is now recognized for what it is. (Dead, Inert, Perfect Waste).

3) So it is with our Spirit (Soul), when it comes time for us to go to Heaven.

4) The Good we have done bears fruit time and time again because it has Roots.

5) The Bad is left behind and forgotten as waste because it has no Roots.

6) Your Spirit (Soul) however, goes to Heaven, Uneffected by the Bad, still "Clean as a Whistle", except for the Aroma of the Good Spice, of course.

7) "Good Word and Deed is the Sugar and Good Thought is the Spice".

8) Also you will note that if you add "Good" Sugar and "Spice" it shows Good judgement and good judgement tells you, you only add "Good " Sugar and Spice" until the water is saturated so as not to waste any water.

9) But if you add a "Bad" Rock, it shows Bad judgement and bad judgement lets you fill the container with "Bad" Rocks, resulting in a lot of waste of water.

10) But luckily not all the water is wasted. There is always some water left in the container.

11) And God, being very flexible, accepts you large or small, sometimes tasty and sometimes not so tasty.

12) So you can see, just as there are many sizes of people in the world, so to there will be many sizes of Bubbles out in Heaven, that Big Big Circle Around Our Magnificent God.

Chapter 14

"Part A"

Reaching Your Full Potential

1) When we set our Everincreasing and Everimproving Goals in Life we want to remember that God always approves of our decisions because God has given us all a separate road to travel and God knows we have to make the Best of what we have.

2) God only says that we follow our instinctive desire to, do Good, bring forth Good producing formulations, and aim to achieve our God given basic purpose in life.

3) Also when we set our Goals (tangible or intangible) we should remember to set them high so that we might reach our full potential. (The Saying is Shoot for the Stars).

4) As we know that if we do not stretch our physical or mental muscle it will not get much stronger. And if we do not stretch out we will not grasp on to our full potential.

5) Consider a Rifle Marksperson, when he/she shoots at a target some distance ahead, he/she always aims higher (more or less depending on the distance) than the target because the bullet drops during its travel.

6) So too, when we set our Goals, we need to set them higher than what we actually need or want because along the road there are always unforeseen obstacles that may lower our results. If no adjustments are forced upon us then we have not lost anything, but gained more.

7) And so while "Shoot for the Stars" is the motto, we must remember that if a rifle marks person shoots with an overly severe incline, he/she will be thrown over backwards when he/she fires the rifle. When this happens the bullet has no chance of striking it's target, but might even fall behind him/her.

8) So too with our Goals in life, we must be realistic (this comes with experience) so as not to aim too high because when we go to apply ourselves, the results are often so far below the mark that we become disillusioned and disappointed to the point where we lose track of our original goal.

9) And if we lose the track of, and the desire for, our goals, we become lost. As a result we often go backward instead of frontward. If this becomes the case, we must start over, aim again and try for a better and wiser attempt.

10) And so a recommended incline is about 39 degrees above the horizon, but this is only relative with each person, (I am about 6'1" tall you see) and also depends upon the direction of the wind.

"Part B"

Re: Goals

11) Our ever-increasing and ever-improving big and good goals are just like little parts of our God, because God is so immense that we cannot begin to define all or the total of God.

12) Since God offers us riches, joy, satisfaction and peace of mind if we set our Goals to the pleasure of God, we should write down, on paper, our Goals so that we can firstly, refer to them for motivation and direction, and secondly, so that we can correctly increase or improve them when and where it is desirable and or necessary.

13) We should set our goals in Two Categories. Firstly, in the Spiritual or Intangible category and secondly, in the Physical or Material category.

14) In the Spiritual category we should list the Traits of Character that we want to acquire or improve upon.

15) And in the Physical or Material category we list the physical or material things we want to acquire or achieve.

16) Now although both categories of Goals are essential in life we should remember that it is the Spiritual or Character advances we make that bring the most and lasting joy and satisfaction. But at the same time we need not neglect the advancement on our physical or material Goals because these are also God's rewards to us for achieving and improving the first category.

17) Now finally, I say, it is absolutely essential that you write down your Goals, specifically, Not just think them, write them down so that you can refer to them, improve upon them, and organize a Step by Step process within certain time frames for and to their achievement.

18) With respect to your "Traits of Character" that you want to acquire or improve upon. You list them and then take one at a time, describe it, on a pocket card, and carry it with you to read while you Practice it for one week. Then take the next trait, describe it and Practice it for one week. Continue the process until you cover them all and repeat until you are strong in them all.

Chapter 15

Positions of Prayer

In the Daytime,

One) Standing up, Head up, Looking up, Eyes open, Eye lids high or low, does not matter, But Eyes open. And if not both, at least the One Eye, Yes, Your Mind's Eye must be open.

Two) On your Bed, (Not under or beside your bed) But on your bed, on your back, Face up, Eyes open, Looking up or out the Window, or to either side, but always in an Upward direction or position. (And Remember, Your Mind's Eye must be open).

Three) Never on your knees; God does not want you

to buckle your knees and not your heart and mind; so you Stand up and Bend your heart and Mind upward.

Four) Never Look down. That is the Shadow you will be Praying to. And that......wants you to Close your eyes too. (The Scum) So you say, Down you .... and put your foot down, and Look up, and Say, Hi, My Dear God, Thank you for my Health and Welfare and for this, that and the other things. And when you are through thanking, you ask God to Always let you remember the Nature of It's Goodness, Love and Forgiveness; Everincreasing and Everimproving, Unconditional and Unconditional. And Dear God always let me Remember to more and more Please you (God), for it is to my advantage.

And if you, occasionally must ask for something more, never ask for anything physical or material, Never, because God will just say, Get off your Heals and go for it, you Jerk. (In this regard, you only thank God for It's Blessing and Approval of your Plans and Goals).

But only and anytime ask for things Spiritual or Mental or of Character Value, anything of this Nature (God's Nature) you will receive, like Zing, within the minute, within the hour, within the day or within the week, not much longer. But right now, you will have it.

And to ensure that you receive your request, Write the request out on paper before you go to bed. And you will be moving with it and for it by morning. And then furthermore, carry the request with you in your shirt pocket, next to your heart and mind, and you will practice it immediately, and when you practice it, you have it. Thank you God, Thank you; Thank you Children, Thank you.

B.H., M.A., L.W.

Poste Script: And one thing more, do not waste your time asking God to do something for someone else, unless you tell that person, What and That you did. So that he/she will eventually, if not immediately, ask When......; And when he/she asks, When?; then you or God will say, When you Ask, my friend, when you ASK; Thank you God Thank you.

B.H., M.A., L.W.

Chapter 16

IF YOU THINK YOU CAN

1) If you think you are beaten, you are;
    If you think you dare not, you don't,
   If you like to win, and don't think you can,
    It's almost a cinch you won't.

2) If you think you'll lose, you're lost,
    For out in the world we find
   Success begins with a person's will;
    It's all in the state of mind.

3) For many a race is lost
    Ere even a step is run,
   And many a coward fails,
    Ere even his/her work is begun.

4) Think big and your deeds will grow,
    Think small and you'll fall behind;
   Think that you can and you will,
    It's all in the state of mind.

5) If you think you are outclassed, you are;
    You've got to think high and rise,
   You've got to be sure of yourself before
    You can ever win a prize.

6) Life's battles don't always go
   To the stronger or faster person,
   But, sooner or later, the person who wins,
   Is the person who thinks he/she can!

7) The above poem is to be given to a poor person just before you give him/her a slice of bread. And if you talk to him/her about It over Lunch, it will not be long before he/she follows you out of the desert and into the Meadow to make some Hay.

oooooOooooo

8) God says, Try Possibilities and become accustomed to Success and the subsequent true, Big as Life Success stories.

   Shadow says, Try Impossibilities and become accustomed to Failure and the subsequent fraudulent, Bigger than Life Counterfeit Miracles.

9) To decipher the Voice of God from the Voice of the Shadow; You ask the Voice to Prove what it is saying. God being the Truth will provide much substantial evidence. Shadow being a Lie provides maybe more Lies, But no evidence. Therefore, Act on the Truth or Discard the Lie, and Worry no more.

Chapter 17

PROVERBS: *(Short, Short Stories)*

The Proverbs of "Saint BILL" son of George and Katherina, farmers of Alberta.. "Saint BILL", was a Real Estate Broker of Alberta

Proverbs 1:

a) If you can not find happiness along the way, do not assume you will find it at the end of the road.

b) If you thing Education is expensive, try Ingnorance.

c) High Heels were invented by a woman who was always kissed on the forehead.

d) God is Singular, but Its actions are Plural, (we, we, we; us, us us; our, our, our) Shadow is Plural, but Its words are Singular, (I, I, I; me, me, me; mine, mine, mine)

e) God says, Speak Up, Shadow says, Speak Down. Because it can only Whisper, the Shadow wants to be heard.

f) God does not speak with words, God speaks with Actions, because Actions speak Louder then words.

g) Love your Family and Friends with All your Heart, but not your Soul because your Soul belongs to God.

h) You may have a Mountain of Faith, But you could not move a Mustard Seed, without first moving your Big toe.

i) If God be with you,
Who can be against you.

j) Drive carefully; Remember,
It is not only a car that can be recalled by its maker.

k) Be Free, Be Happy go Lucky,
Life is a Joke, Not a Yoke.

l) Speak the Truth, It sets you Free,
The Truth is, You are Free

m) A person who can not take Criticism is not very Strong, Confident or Broad in Mind or in Character.

n) God is a Mathematical Genius,
    Yes, God is Logical and Truth.
    Shadow is a Theoretical Moron,
    Yes, Shadow is Illogical and Lie.

o) To be Free is to be Sane,
    Sanity has its Guidelines,
    Insanity knows no Guidelines.

p) If you have a Score to settle,
    You must do it before bedtime,
    Because you do not let the Sun
    go down on your wrath.

q) Start each day in the Initiative
    Not in the negative of Response.

r) God sees and plans for Tomorrow (the Future)
    But only tells about Today (the Present)
    The Good of Yesterday, having Roots,
    We respond to in the Positive today,
    The Bad of Yesterday, having no Roots,
    We do and should Forget. (Forgive)

s) To Believe is to Obey,
    To Obey is to gain "Applied Faith"
    to Procrastinate is to gain "Blind Faith"

PROVERBS 2:

a) "The Spirit of Goodness" verses "The Hoity-Toity Spirit" There are two types of Enthusiasm, one is a bouncing rubber ball, the other is a big Bubble ready to burst at the first sign of trouble.

Illustration:

The Previewlite says, This coming year I will do this, this, and that.
This coming month I will do this, this, and that.
And God has approved my plans and goals, Oh Boy, am I Enthusiastic!
The Shadow-worshipper says, Hey, If I do not doubt, I can walk on water. Oh Boy, Am I Enthusiastic!

As you can see one is based on truth and reality.
The other is based on lie and illusion.
One is a recipe for success., the other a recipe for failure.
Yes, one Rebounds from every obstacle and keeps going.
The other takes One step forward and.. "Splash",, and the Enthusiasm goes "Poof".

b) All things are possible Except those which are against God's Laws of Nature.

c) No-one can break God's Laws of Nature, Except the Shadow. And the reason the Shadow can break God's Laws of Nature is because It lies.

d) Today,....Well Lived,
Makes every yesterday,..A Dream of Happiness And every Tomorrow,... A Vision of Hope.

e) The Dictionary is the only place where Success comes before Work.

f) Criticism is something you can avoid by saying nothing, doing nothing, and being nothing.

g) Flexibility is the cornerstone of Progress

h) To Direct Change, you must be out front: to be and remain out front, you must (Bend) Adapt to Change quickly without breaking your train of Thought.

i) Behold the Turtle, It does not make progress unless It sticks Its neck out.

j) If something is worth doing,
It is worth doing well.

PROVERBS 3:

a) There are two types of Fictional writings (stories), One is within the Realms of Possibilities, The other is outside of beyond the Realms of Possibilities.
So if you are presented with the first type, Read it and enjoy it without fear of harm, because it is within the Realms of Possibilities. But if you are presented with the other type, avoid it if possible or at the least do not take it seriously, because it is outside or beyond the Realms of Possibilities. They all add up to, Hey, if you do not doubt, you can walk on water. And then they have the gall to say, Believe me, It is Reality. Wrong, It is Illusion, which if you believe, is designed to disintegrate your sense of Judgement. So that you do not know right from wrong, true from false or good from bad, and ultimately renders you an Imbecile. So just say, Thanks but No thanks, I need something that will keep my sense of balance Intact.

b) Thank you Dear God,
For Sun and Shower
Thank you,..For each Lovely Flower
Thank you, For each Stately Tree
Through all these,.. You Speak to me.

c) Recall it as often as you want,
A happy moment never wears out.

d) There is no use saying, I Forgive you,
If you are unwilling to Forget.

e) Those who do a Kindness and are not in some way Thanked, Seem to forget to do it again.

f) Instead of Dreaming about Loving your Enemies, Face Reality, and Treat your Friends a bit Better. yes, Practice first,... Then comes Excellence

g) You can have only two things in Life,
Reasons or Results, and
Reasons do not Count.

h) FAITH is the Glue between Thought and Action. If you Act the Glue gells (Solidifies) and you become a stronger person and gain "Applied Faith".
But if you Procrastinate the Glue waters down and you become weak in Character and gain "Blind Faith".

i) FORGIVING is a selfish Act,
The One it helps most, is you.
So do it Often, Quickly and Easily.
And It lets Love grow.

A Metaphor

j) These are the Times of The "Steel Glass
  Balls"
The "Stones of Truth"
Throw them often, they are,
"Steel Glass, Not Crystal"
"Well Tempered, Not Frozen"
Yes, Steel Glass, My Friends, is
"Getting harder than Rock" But
"STILL flexible", Tempered not Frozen.
You can hit it as Hard as you want with a
Sledge Hammer and it "Will not Break". It
will "Bend but not Break". It may be
Unconscious, but it "Will not be out Cold". It
will Obsorbe the Shock, and Recover. yes,
"Steel Glass" is "One-Clean-Clear-Through"
"Not a crack in It".
Throw it down hard and "Never a crack".
"Firm but Flexible" " Strong and Potent"
Waiting to Fly, But Eager to Rebound.
Just like a Golf Ball, only,
"One-Clean-Clear-Through
"Bounces like a Kingman....Flies like a Bird.
And smashes Illusions like CREAM PUFF PIE

PROVERBS 4:

a) If you Think good, You See Good.
If you Think Bad, You See Bad.
God does not Think Bad, Therefore
God Sees No Bad in the World,
Only Good and Some Waste.

b) God's Cup (container) in you, always grows as your goodness grows, and therefore is always Replenished and Full, But never Runs Over; Unless you Lie, Steal, Kill, or Overindulge. You might say, God cries a little for you because of the waste, every time you add a Bad Rock. (Ch. 13, P.92) Now if you add too many Bad Rocks too quickly, the Cup becomes full of Bad Rocks and God stops crying; Until you do One of Two things. You either stop doing bad things to give the Goodness left in you a chance to grow again to slowly overcome the Bad again, or You Rot in Jail and pay the Penalty the Shadow hands out the hard way. God all the while stands by and takes you into Heaven if or when you die in Jail; A little small, mind you, but none the less a Humanbeing.

c) God does not fear
God does not instill Fear.
Therefore we should not fear
And we should not instill Fear.
It Follows That,
One should not Act out of Fear
And One should not Fear to Act.

d) People who come to Think God requires a sacrifice, have come to think a Lie
And soon stop worshipping.

e) A person who comes to Think God requires Obedience, is on the Road of Truth and soon learns to say Thank you for my Blessings my Dear God

f) People who have no Faith in others
Have very little Faith in themselves.

g) My Summit is my Home & My Home is my Summit, and My Congregation is My Family.

h) Old age is not so Bad,
when you consider the Alternative

i) Have Faith in your "God of Good",
And It will be your Servant,
But do not Waver,
Lest You drop the Blessings

PROVERBS 5:

a)   God brings forth Truth
        Shadow brings forth Lie.
        Truth brings forth Ideas
        Lie brings forth Illusions.
        Ideas bring forth Possibilities
        Illusions bring forth Impossibilities.
        Possibilities bring forth Success
        Impossibilities bring forth Failure.
        Success brings forth Success Stories
        Failure brings forth Counterfeit Miracles.

b)   Experience leads to Reality
        Reality leads to Moderation
        Moderation leads to Balance
        Balance leads to Good Judgement
        Good Judgement leads to Good Actions
        Good Actions lead to Blessings
        Blessings lead to "Thanks to God".
        Thanks to God leads to "A Pleased God"
        A Pleased God leads to a Healthy Mind.

c) Inaction leads to Fantasy
Fantasy leads to Extremes
Extremes leads to Lies
Lies lead to Confusion
Confusion leads to Poor Judgement
Poor Judgement leads to Bad Actions
Bad Actions lead to Punishment
Punishment leads to Denial
Denial leads to "A Laughing Shadow"
A Laughing Shadow leads to a Sick Mind.

d) Counterfeit Miracles bring forth Despair
Despair brings forth Self-inflicted-Pain
Self-inflicted-Pain brings forth a Bad Slow Death.

e) Success Stories bring forth Hope
Hope brings forth Enthusiasm
Enthusiasm brings forth a Good Fast Life.

f) Yeh, Yeh, Yeh to Success Stories and
To Hell with Counterfeit Miracles.

g) There are two kinds of Thought
One is Practical: One is Impractical
The Practical we shall call Idea
The Impractical we shall call Illusion
One is a product of Truth
One is a product of Lie.
God speaks with Actions, therefore
brings forth the Practical
Shadow speaks Without Actions, therefore
brings forth the Impractical.

h) God is very Great in Thought, Word and Deed. There are 5.1 Billion people in the World today, including men, women and children. And if we took all the Wisdom and interpretations of the wisdom of God, of all 5.1 Billion people and put it all together, We would still only have the equivalent of "One Balloon Full" of knowledge out of the Universe of God's Knowledge. But Nonetheless, it would be a "Loving Force" to be Reckoned with if All brought in Line.

i) God never Says,. I Love you,. because
    Its' Actions Prove it.
Shadow never Says,. I Hate you,. because
    that would be the Truth
And that is impossible to come from the
    Shadow

j)   A Seed is in an Apple, An Apple is in a Tree,
A Tree is in a Root, A Root is in a Seed,
A Seed is in a Root, A Root is in a Tree,
A Tree is in an Apple, An Apple is in a Seed.

(Yes, One yet One in All)

What we must remember is,
"Where are the Roots"

In the Sky or in the Ground
If in the Ground then we have Lie,
as Lie is as in Darkness.
If in the Sky then we have Truth,
as Truth is as in Light.

It is said that:
The Apple does not Fall
Far from the Tree.

Therefore, we know we are none of the Negative. We are God's Children which sees or knows no Bad in us. We just Stumble ove rthe Shadow once in a while, But God sees it coming and says, Forgiven or Not Guilty. (Thank you, Dear God, Thank you.)

PROVERB 6:

a) Some people say, I sin against God. (Offend Against God)
Some people say, I am Perfect.
Some people say both in the same breath.
(All three are to the pleasure of the Shadow)

b) <u>On the first part,</u> The Shadow just loves to have you think you sin against God, because that separates you from God and leaves you in the hands of the Shadow; And the Shadow just drives you into the ground with guilt, confusion and hate.

c) The fact is, you do not sin against God, you sin against your fellow humanbeings. Yes, remember, God and you are on the same side; And remember god is not Perfect, God is

d) Therefore, God set you Free to "Reap what you Sow" and because you are at times looking down to the Shadow you are incorrectly influenced at times and subsequently you Offend against Humanity, not against God. Remember, God is never Offended by anyone and God is never alienated from anyone; God is Everunderstanding and Evermercyfull, Everloving.

e) Therefore, remember that after the Offence, You look Up, and God says, Forgiven; Then God says, Now ask and you shall receive the strength and you will exercise the strength that I have given you to overcome the influence of the Shadow the next time you cross a similiar path.

f) <u>On the second part.</u> The Shadow just loves to hear you say, I am Perfect, because you are then in Its hands. You are then finished, complete, with out further room for improvement, finite, resting like a rock, inert, standing still, doing nothing, no where to go. Hopeless, helpless. Do you get the picture, the Shadow would just laugh to Hell and back if It could just get someone, anyone to such a hopeless situation.

g) But do not despair, God will not allow it, God has, does and will always intervene, because God always has an Army of Helpers who come and touch you on the shoulder and say, Look Up and to the Right. Come, this way and you will do just fine.

h) <u>On the third part.</u> It is obvious that this is to the pleasure of the Shadow. I need say no more, right, right, Right. (Excepting as God would say, to Hell with the Shadow, Out into outer Darkness, beyond the reach of Light, and stay there, I need you there for reference.)

PROVERBS 7:

a)   There are some people who try to Reduce God to a Human. There are some people who try to Raise Humans to God. Both are to the pleasure of the Shadow.

On the first part the Shadow just loves to see someone try to Reduce God because It is so jealous of God. (and Frustrated too, eh.)

On the second part the Shadow would just love to see anyone and everyone suffer and die a Lunatic because Suffer and Lunacy are the Names of Its Game. (ref. Ch. 9vs. 16 P.76)

b)   God and Its relation to people can be likened to a "City Water-Works System". For instance in "Calgary" we have the Glenmore Reservoir. A large body of water up to a Dam. From the Reservoir we have the Water Mains and from the Water Mains we go to the Half-inch tap. Well, the Half-inch pipe in the kitchen can be considered "Gods Waiting Hand". From the tap flows God's Love and Instruction. Some people leave the tap closed, some go once in a while for a Love touch on the head, Others leave it drip.

Others go quite regularly for a word of advice, and finally some learn to leave the tap on continually at a speed their personal composure can endure. (That is the first stage, Now for the second).

c) As mentioned some people try to Reduce God to a Human, so they phone City Hall and say turn Down the pressure. The City says, sorry, there are too many people depending on God to please just you. So you will have to accept God as It is or turn off the tap, and if you wish you can seal it with Sodder, but we can not Reduce the pressure to please you. The pressure has been on too long to change now. Yes, it is fixed except for fluctuations. (That was stage Two Now for number Three).

d) As mentioned some people try to Raise Humans to God, so they go and buy a Two-Foot watermain pipe Two-Foot long. They then proceed to try to attach it to the Half-inch tap. After much A-Do they finally give up and turn on the tap as it is. They then turn on the tap full-blast. After sometime they phone City Hall and say, turn Up the pressure, we want and need more Love and Instruction. The City says, Sorry, we can not turn up the pressure because it will break the pipes.

And when the pipes break it is a Mad house. So the pressure has to stay the same because its been set too long and it is fixed except for fluctuations. Besides, if you get more Instruction than full-blast, you go insane. Then these people say, I do not believe you, I will go to the Reservoir. So off they go to the Reservoir, and when they get there they say, not enough and no pressure, Where is the source? And so up the river they go until they reach a little Trickle out of the mountain side. Now they have time to think and it is cold and windy, and soon they go back home and leave the tap on a Trickle. (That was those that learn easy; Some jump into the Reservoir and drown; Others go Mad and stay Mad; Still others commit suicide.) (Thus the saying, "You can not fight City Hall).

e) And so to summarize we say, God is Greater than your comprehension and in fact the size of the Universe of Universes, but all we get is the Stem of God's Umbrella, God's waiting hand. So you surround yourself with your God's hand and continue your walk with God, stopping twice a day, once in the morning and once in the evening, to read a little from "The Compass". It is not a Two-foot water main pipe, with Two thousand pages to confuse or drown you.

It is a Half-inch Tap with 287 punch packed pages of Truth and Reality to keep you "Free on Track and Enthused. God Bless you,

            ooooo0ooooo

The Prayer of "Saint Bill"
(All together now, too.)

My Dear God in Heaven, In the World,
And in my Heart, Mind and Soul,
I Love you, I Love you, and I,
Thank you for "The Compass," for
Thy Kingdom has come by it and
Thy Will, is now done on Earth as it is in Heaven.
Let us remember to "Look Up' in our daily activities
Let us forgive one another as thou hast forgiven us
Thank you for letting me remember to everyday more
and more please you, for it is to my advantage
Thank you for my daily Bread
Thank you for my Health and Well Being
In Spirit, Body and Mind
Thank you for All my Blessings
Thank you for my Family and Friends
Thank you for making me Happy go Lucky
Thank you for Reserving a Spot for me in Heaven,
Dear God,
Thank you for All things Good
For Thine is the Kingdom, the Power and the Glory,
for ever and Ever.
Amen, Amen and Amen

Chapter 18

Closing Remarks

1) The Good nature of God, Its unconditional Love and Its unconditional Forgiveness and the philosophy that comes (coincides) with it shall be and remain intangible and Universally acceptable.

2) God, Its Philosophy, Its plan and Its purpose has been Revealed by Human Genius, because God is Intangible. God does not speak out loud, It does not write books. God has no Physical Characteristics at all. God only has Spiritual, Mental, Emotional or Psychological characteristics.

3) The Insight, Revelation or Definition of Our Universal God and philosophy is not now and is not ever to be claimed to be inspired, as though written by God. Because that type of claim at anytime is not an innocent misconception, but rather, a conscious Lie and We are looking up not down.

4) The Application or implementation of this philosophy and the Will of God shall be carried out by the same motivation that a parent has

to teach and show its children what is Good in God's Eye and what brings riches, joy, satisfaction and peace of mind in the Tangible an Intangible things of Life and in the inner and outer self of Life. This motivation is inherent in all of us, at any age level, and whatever knowledge we have to pass on in the field of Our God and this philosophy of life, came to us for free and shall be passed on for free; As parents do not expect to be paid for teaching and showing their children of these facts of life.

5) For the purpose of communal gatherings, larger scale gatherings and gatherings for the purpose of praise and worship there shall be democratically elected Leaders and democratically elected Assistants to expand the sphere and effectiveness of the leaders. These leaders (Promoters of this philosophy and Will of our god) shall be elected from the "Root People of Society". And remember the tree is Upside Down. This means that the emphasis shall be on practical (Experienced) knowledge, not on theoretical knowledge. Therefore, nominees for leadership will be approximately Forty (40) years old or older and will naturally be inclined to now share their experience and knowledge both

in the tangible and intangible forms, for the improvement and advancement of all Human kind.

6) And now, I come to declare my position in all this regard. I believe and know there is a place Reserved for me in that Big Big Circle around our Magnificient God. To be more specific, I say, I believe and know that I am already in the Circle......(The Family of God) of the past, the present and unto Eternity.

7) I declare this, and take this position, not by my own, but because I believe it is the Will of my God that I declare and take my position in Its Eternal Heavenly plan of the past, the present and the Infinite future.

8) And on one side of me, I see Confucius, Buddha, Jefferson, Victoria,...... and on the other side of me, I see Sitting Bull, Muhammad, Gorbachev,...... and even Moses, ...and then.... Well, Well,......I'll be "Blessed not Damned",....Cassius Clay, alias Muhammad Ali, the man who dances like a buttefly and stings like a Bee. There is a man after my own heart, The Greatest, Yes my dear God, the Greatest

9) And so to complete the picture I simply ask your understanding and forgiveness, for not having the room on this page to list all the remaining nations and cultures of the world, but I assure you and I know you know that you are All present and Tall.

10) And now directly across the expanse, I see my family (immediate and otherwise) starting with my wife, Leola, and all the Jones, then my father and mother, Katherina and Georg, my brothers and sister, Theophil, Arthur I, Arthur 2, Alfred, Salvin, and Hilda. My daughter and Sons, Evelyn, Gregory, Vincent and Rex. My nephews, and nieces, my cousins, my Uncles and Aunts, They are all there. And of course <u>All of you are in too.</u>

11) And in the infinitely expanding circle around our Immense and Diverse God and Its universe of universes, there is room for all of Human kind of the past, the present and of the Eternity. <u>All in the Outermost Circle,</u> rejoicing, observing, and singing praises unto Our Magnificient God of Good, Love and Forgiveness.

12) And Now I say to you, This is your compass and road map, the Final Testament, and is of the True God of Good, Love and Forgiveness,

that has always been here with us. It just took God a while to find someone to put it down in writing. Butnow it is here (and that is what matters).

13) Submitted to you and yours and All of Humankind (the World over) for your individual and collective use and guidance unto the Eternity of Humankind (forever).

14) The Ball is rolling and it will not be long before it overtakes all the Six corners of this world (called Earth).

15) Thank you, Dear God, Thank you,

With Love and Forgiveness to All of Humankind
(Unconditionally)

W. J. (Bill) Handel, M.A., L.W.
(Alias: "Saint Bill")
Deist, a believer of and in Deism
The Universal God in Its Finest form (Intangible)
As Defined by Human Genius.

54 B.H. M.A., L.W.,
5939 A.M.

Poste Script:

> You will note that the colours of the cover around the COMPASS are green and Blue. That is because it seems to me that God's favourite colours are Green and Blue. Yes, GREEN Grass and BLUE Skies.

oooooOooooo

You will note that the Pages of the COMPASS are printed on one side only.

That is because God's face is always away from you and looking Forward to the Future, and what ever may come its way; And God's word is written on Its Back facing you. So when you turn and step into the stem of God's Umbrella, God's word becomes written on Your Back; And so God's word Shines backwards and Drives the Shadow away out to outer Darkness beyond the Reach of Light.

And God's Face is in front of you, but of course, Still Looking to the Future.

Thank you God Thank you.

B.H., M.A., L.W.

PosteScript:

Ref. Ch. 2 v. 54; God says, All my children, Yellow, Red, Black, White and Brown, throughout the world will meet me in Heaven. (the Rich, the Poor, the Good and the Seemingly Bad).

Shadow says, only you who watch me will go to Heaven. Yes, I will take you there personally and introduce you.

"Saint Bill" agrees with God and says, All of Humankind goes to Heaven. It is a Spiritual Reality that we wake up to when we pass-on. Because God, with Its infinite wisdom would not have created a Universe and Manifested Itself in the Human mind without creating a Heaven as the "Last Vacation Destination".

"Saint Bill" further says, and clarifies that you All will go to Heaven, Head-Up or Head-Down and respectively, with or without "Saint Bill"; But if you want to enjoy a little bit of Heaven right here on Earth as God meant it to be, Head-up, then you can be assured you will do just Fine with "Saint Bill"; Because you are Free of any Physical, Mental or Spiritual impairments and can expend your energies to the fullest extent toward the achievement of your "God Approved" goals in Life.

Therefore, just as it is a Certainty that we All meet in Heaven, So it is a Certainty that the "Spirit of Saint Bill" has, does, and will Live Forever in the Hearts, Minds and Souls of the Past, Present and Future generations, because. It is the "Free Spirit of God", yes, "The Spirit of goodness", with all of its children (angels), the oldest being "The Spirit of Truth" and the youngest being "The Spirit of Enthusiasm", with many inbetween as manifested in and by "The COMPASS" which is now a Reality.

So, The Glory be to God,
Thank you, Children and Friends, Thank you.
Thank you, Dear God, Thank you.

B.H., M.A., L.W.

THE
COMPASS
Supplement # 1

The Letter of The Truth
The Whole Truth and
Nothing But The Truth
So Help Me God

by:

W.J. (Bill) Handel, M.A., L.W.
Alias: "Saint BILL"

Dear Friends in "Saint BILL"
At "Previews" we take a Realistic approach with our Dear God.
No Fantasy, No Illusion and NO Lies. Just Truth and Reality. Before these presence, if you were amoungst those that grew up without the benefit of Religion, you were probably lucky. Because there are two types of Religion. Yes there is Theology and there is Philosophy. Theology is based on Theory, unproven, impractical Theory or Supposition. While Philosophy is based on Reality or proven, practical principals.

Yes, Theology portrays a super natural God or an unnatural, unrealistic God. While Philosophy portrays a Natural God or a Realistic God. Now we all know God is Natural not Unnatural. The unnatural God is constantly doing the impossible, but with words only, No Actions or Results to show. The Natural God pays no attention to the impossible. It is too busy doing the possible or realistic things of life.

Yes, everything we have or do in life is to the Glory of the Natural God. Why, because if God had not manifested Itself in the Human mind we would be nothing more than animals. But God manifested in us Its Sense of Judgement, (the Calculating ablility
referred to in Ch.1,v.13), that being a sense of Right and wrong and a sense of Good or Bad.

And so all the Good we have and all the Good we do is to the Glory of God. The Truthfull, Realistic, Natural God. Not the lieing, unrealistic, unnatural God. Yes, folks we can Relate to the Natural God, but we can not Relate to the Unnatural God; because the Natural God is Real, while the Unnatural God is Illusion.

Yes, the Natural God says, Feed and water your Cattle and you will soon have more Cattle., and Zap nine months later, more Cattle. Glory to God. The Natural God says, Plant some wheat and you will soon have more wheat., and Zap, four months later, more wheat. Glory to God, right. The Natural God says, Pour some metal and you will soon have more cars., and Zap, two months later, ten thousand more cars. Thanks and Glory to God for Enginuity........

.... Now the Unnatural God says, Have no Doubt and you can walk on water. And zap, one step forward and Splash.., Glory to God, right, Yes, thank God, God will not allow anyone to break Its Laws of nature. Gods' Laws of Nature are fixed; No-one can break them unless they lie. And of course when we lie anything is possible.

But Thank God, God is not Quite Allmighty, Almost but not Quite. (99999/100000) Thank God, God can not do Everything. Thank God, God can not Kill, God can not Lie, God can not Steal, God can not Move a Mountain, by saying Mountain move. God can not walk on water, God can not Raise the Dead; God can not Condemn anyone, and God can not Tempt us to do Bad. God can not Compromise or Deal in any way with the Shadow.

Yes, God can not break Its own Laws of nature, Thank God, or we would not have a God anymore we would have a Two-Faced Hypocrite.

Thank God, That as it is, we have God and the Shadow of God; Which is a Helpless, Hopeless Mr. Nothing, if we "Look Up" in our daily activities.

Thank you, Dear God, Thank you, for Philosophy,
The Philosophy of:
"Previews Institute of Universal Philosophy"
as Founded by "The Compass"
which draws a clear line between Truth and Lie, Reality and Illusion, Good and Waste, God and
Shadow And stays on the side of the Natural, Truthfull, the Good and the Real God of life.

Thank you Dear God, Thank you.
B.H., M.A.., L.W.
Alias: Saint BILL"

THE MELTING POT,... continued

18) Thank God, god is all Good, but not perfect. God is alive, Active and good. Ever Increasing, Ever Improving, Excellent, Flexilble, Easily Pleased and Far Far ahead of you. God is Unconditionally Loving, Unconditionally Forgiving, Ever Understanding, and Ever Merciful.

Yes, Thank God, God is not Perfect, God is not finished, Complete, Without further room for Improvement, Finite, Resting like a Rock, Inert, Standing still, Doing nothing, No-where to go, Helpless, Hopeless.

Yes, Thank God, God is All Good and will always have somewhere to go, something to do. Always Hopefull of the Future and Regenerating. Thank God.

oooooOooooo

19 We all know that God does not Tempt, Test, Encourage, Lead or Suggest that we do some thing bad. we all know it is the Shadow which Tempts, Tests, Encourages, Leads and Suggests we do Bad things.

Yet there are people who say that God would go so far as to Tempt a person to Kill. Can you imagine that; God says, thou shalt not Kill. That is Evil.

So you can see, it is obvious that these people are calling the wrong Spirit God.

oooooOooooo

20) We all know that God, Thinks no Bad, Sees no Bad, Hears no Bad, Knows no Bad, and Does no Bad. Yet there are some people who say that God would go so far as to send out Evil Spirits to cause problems and disharmony amoungst Its people. Well, we all know it is the Shadow that does that in the form of more Illusions and Lies; And it is obvious that these people have mistaken the Shadow for God, and in effect are worshipping the Shadow, not God at all.

oooooOooooo

21) Dear is My Gods' name, Yes, My Gods' name is Dear to me.

What is your Gods' name?,......Well some people call their God Allah, some say Mohhammed, some say Buddha and so on.

All very well and Good. But can you imagine calling your God Jealous. Well what an insult to God.

To call God Love is to call It a "Good Spirit", but to call God Jealous is to call It an "Evil Spirit". Yes, Love is a Good Spirit and Jealousy is an Evil Spirit, just as Hate is an Evil Spirit.

Yes, I have heard of people who call their God Jealous and when asked, Why, they say there is such a thing as Righteous Jealousy. Can you imagine that, Righteous Jealousy. That is like Comprimizing with the Shadow and saying there is Righteous Sin; Now we all know that is not a go with God and it is obvious that these people have been confused.

oooooOooooo

22) Question,...... How is it that some people worship a Two-Faced God. Yes, I noticed on one side It is all green and wrinkled, and on the other side It is as smooth as a Babys'.

On the Left side they worship an Evil old man,... On the Right side they worship a Perfect young Lunatic. (A Cripple yet) Can not walk on its own, It needs the Old man to be the Crutch.

One is all Jealous and the other is all Love, and love is not Jealous. One lies and the other swears to it. No room for Truth in either one.

oooooOooooo

23) Gods' road of life for you does not have Rocks (Boulders) in your path.
If you find a Rock in your path it usually means the road is a Dead End Street. Now, if you can see over the Rock then make arrangements to go around the Rock and continue on your way. But if you can not see over the Boulder, then do not let your perserverance waste your energy trying to move the Boulder.

Use your better Judgement and change Direction to the Right. You will always find your new Direction and road is a New and better opportunity and a step forward not backward.

oooooOooooo

24) ATTITUDE: The Positive and the Negative.
A cup can be either Half Full or Half Empty.
God says, you are Half Full, you are Something and Somebody.
Shadow says, you are Half Empty, you are Nothing and Nobody.
God says, you are 1/4 full, you are really a Somebody.
Shadow says, you are 3/4 empty, you are really a Nothing and a Nobody.
God says, you are 3/4 full, you are really really Somebody.
Shadow says, you are 1/4 empty, you are still a Nothing and Nobody.
It is obvious which is the Positive way to look at things.

oooooOooooo

25) There are two types of Religion. One is Theology and One is Philosophy. Theology is based on Theory, Unproven impractical theory. Philosophy is based on Principals, Proven practical principals. in other words, One is based on truths and reality and the other is based on suppositions or illusions.

Take for example the supposition of, "Turn the other cheek 700 times". What would you have if you applied that theory,....Well go ahead tell me,..... (no answer).... Well I will tell you,......You would have One Big Bully and one Mashed Wimp.

Now let us look at a proven principal,.... God says, In the Initiative Treat others as you would like to be Treated. but in the Response, Treat others as they Treat you, and even more so. That is to say, that if someone treats you Good, you treat them Better. And if someone treats you Bad, you treat them Worse.

So the Principal is "Never strike the first Blow", because if you strike the first Blow, you get Two back; Now what do you have when you apply that Principal. Well go ahead tell me,...... (no answer).... Well I will tell you,.... You have no Wimps and no Bullies,... Just Respect for one another and peace on Earth.
("Saint BILL" is called the "King of Peace".)

26) Theology vs. Philosophy:
There are some people who say they have a Perfect Story for Salvation. The problem is the Foundation is false. The Foundation is that God Condemned the First man and woman for being led astray by the Shadow.

Well, we know that God does not Condemn anyone, God Forgives. Therefore the whole story is an excercise in futility; Because man and woman are not (condemned to be) born with a Bad nature. They are born with a Good nature (Gods' Nature) by nature. And as such, Salvation is our God Given Birth-Right.

Question:

1) Where are the First man and woman,... In heaven with God or In Hell with the Shadow. (In Heaven of course, because Hell has only room for one)

2) When did they go to Heaven,... When they died or fifty thousand years later. (When they died of course, the Shadows fairy tale is just Illusion)

God has always had, has, and always will have, a spot reserved in Heaven for each and every one of us when we die physically; And our Spirit does not die but goes to Heaven immediately. Because God is Evermercyfull and Everforgiving It made no arrangements for a big Hell. God did not plan for a Hell, It just Planned a Heaven for us All. The Shadow was just a bit of unexpected Waste that showed up.

So God put It in a little box (a One inch cube of Vacuum) and sent It out into outer Darkness, beyond the reach of Light, and said, Stay there, I need you there for reference.

oooooOooooo

27) There are some people who say that Human kind is born without a Nature, neither Good or Bad. But develop either a Good nature or a Bad nature.

Well that may be so, but I will tell you of something Humankind is born with that no-one can argue with . Humankind is born with a Sense of Judgement and you can use your Sense of Judgement or let it waste away and be an Imbecile all your life. But if you use your Sense of Judgement, being your sense of right and wrong, you will naturally choose your Good nature over the Bad, because you know that Good brings Joy and Satisfaction and bad Brings Sorrow and Dissatisfaction. So there you go, you have a Good nature as a result of your Sense of judgement, by Nature. It is just a matter of which comes first, the Chicken or the Egg. Now we know that no-one knows the answer to that, but we do know they go together

Now you know why the Shadow says, "Do not Judge". Yes, It wants you to stay an Imbecile all your life so that you do not get ahead of It. Dirty play, Dirty pool. Yes, the Shadow is not completely stupid, just Dirty, Dirty. Playing in the Mud. Always playing in the Mud.

oooooOooooo

28)   There are some people who say that God did not intend for us to know right from wrong, and that we be just like the Animals. Well, how ridiculous. Of course God intended for us to know right from wrong, BUT, BUT after our Decisions and Judgements regarding the words and actions of people, God wants us to always say "Not Guilty" or "Forgiven", and then give the other person the alternative route, as God does, and in this way gradually bring the other person to God's way of thinking instead of the Shadows', which is to not know right from wrong and be an Imbecile or a Condemning Slave driver.

oooooOooooo

(29)

Dear Friends in "Saint Bill",

We all know that it is Universally believed and accepted that God is Good, God is Truth, God is Love, God is Tolerance and many more such good and wonderfull Characteristics. And we also know that it is Universally believed and accepted that God has not, does not and will not ever Condemn anyone, but that God Forgives.

Therefore, when someone says to you, You are all Condemned, Cursed, Bewitched and so on; We know who is speaking do we not; Yes, the Shadow of course and It is a Powerless Lier from the very beginning, trying to pull a Guilt trip over you in order to gain your allegiance and furthermore your Sacrifices.

But from the very beginning we have been blessed with a Loving God, a Forgiving God, a Truthfull God and a Real God; Not a Hatefull, Vengefull, Lieing, Illusion of a God; And Thank God we are not Condemned to be born with a Bad nature but rather we are Blessed to be born with a Good Nature (Gods nature) by nature.

And because we are born with a Good nature, Gods nature, (and Gods nature is all of Good), we need not worry about our Salvation. It has never been in question. We know God is always in charge of

Its affairs and set us Free from the beginning to Go and Come again without Guilt or Sacrifice to take our place in that spot reserved for each and every one of us when our Spirits pass on into Heaven. Yes Folks, Thank God, Salvation is our God given Birth-Right. Because God did not plan for a Hell, It just planned for a Heaven for us All. The Bad guy (The Shadow) was just a bit of unexpected Waste that showed up. So God put It in a little box (a one inch cube of Vacuum) and sent It out into outer Darkness, beyond the reach of light, and said, stay there, I need you there for reference.

Yes Folks, the Question is not Salvation to Heaven, (that is a Given),the Question is Salvation on Earth. Bringing Heaven to Earth so that you can enjoy a little of Heaven right here on Earth.

So the Question is do you "Look Up" or do you " Look Down"during your daily activities. If you "Look Up" you see Truth and Reality and become Enthused. If you " Look Down" you see Illusions and Lies and become Depressed......,

So there you go, you have no choice, you must "Look Up" and see Truth and Reality which leads to Opportunity and Opportunity leads to Accomplishment, Now Accomplishment leads to Self-Respect and Pride based on Results; And this is what God wants of you, "Pride in Accomplishment" and Enthusiasm; Happiness, which is a result of successfully serving.

Yes, it has been mentioned before, but Gods' Purpose is to make you Happy, Proud and Happy and keep you free of Guilt, Fear, Doubt and Illusion.

And so we Thank God there is really no choice because the alternative is a humiliated Triflers Pain.

So to sum up, we say "Look Up" and Hear and See the Actions of God and then follow suit in producing "Good" for your fellow Humanbeings.

Thank you Dear God Thank you.
B.H., M.A., L.W.
Alias: "Saint BILL".

P.S.: Remember, when the Clouds come, Do not Look Down; Continue Looking up as you Visualize (Realize) the Sun is still Shining above the Clouds.

B.H., M.A., L.W., Alias: "Saint Bill"

PROVERBS
OF
" Saint BILL"
Short, Short Stories

Continued

PROVERBS 8

a) At Night, My God watches in over me.
By Day, my God watches out for me.

b) If you get a Perfect Idea, It is an Illusion, because Real Ideas need to be Worked out with always some chips or waste falling by the wayside.

c) The Evil Spirit is an Illusion because It is Lie.
The Good Spirit is Real because It is Truth.

d) I would rather Deal with a Sheep in a Wolfes skin, Than to Deal with a Wolfe in a Sheep skin.

e) Previewlites live by their Philosophy because it is Truth and Truth is possible.
Other Profess a Theology but do not live by It because it is Lie, and Lie is impossible.
One is a Straight shooter, The other is a Hypocrite.

f) The Truth once written is always an obvious and easy choice.

g) The Birth of Reality is The Death of Illusion.

PROVERBS 9

a) God is very Great in Thought (Spirit) and not totally comprehendable, because it is a Free Spirit. But the God we see is our Self-Image. If we see ourselves as a Good person then we Act Good. If we see ourselves as a Bad person then we Act Bad. It follows that if we Act Bad we reinforce and increase our Bad image. And if we Act Good we reinforce and increase our Good image.

b) But since Actions start with Ideas, we must encourage our Self-Image to the Good and Better, and our Actions will become Good and better. Then in the process our God becomes a Better and Better God. On the other hand if we think we are Bad our God becomes worse and worse. So it is obvious that it is better to believe you are born with a Good Nature in the likeness of God than to say you are born with a Bad Nature in the likeness of the Shadow

c) So to conclude we say, anyone who says we are born with a Bad Nature is serving the Shadow. And anyone who says we are born with a Good Nature is serving God.

And ultimately we know that if we serve the Shadow we are serving ourselves, which leads to poverty in every way. But if we serve God we are serving others, which leads to riches in every way. Thank you, Dear God, Thank you, for an obvious and easy choice.

PROVERBS 10

a) Every Human being in the world, of the past, present and future, is born a "Previewlite", Yes, a child of God. And as a child of God, He/She is born with Two things; A sense of Judgement and a Good Nature. The sense of Judgement is the chicken and the Good Nature is the Egg inside the chicken. And so as your sense of Judgement develops so does your GoodNature.

b) Because your sense of Judgement tells you "Good" brings Joy and Satisfaction and "Bad" brings Sorrow and Dissatisfaction, you naturally choose the "Good", which in turn develops your Good Nature. The sense of Judgement and the Good Nature are inseparable and always develop together.

c) Now you know why the Shadow says "Do not Judge", Yes, It knows it can not destroy you, because God Forgives, So the Shadow just attempts to waste you.

PROVERBS 11

a) God has a "Free Spirit", a "Sense of Judgement", and a "Good Nature".
It is the "Sense of Judgement" that guides your "Free Spirit" in a straight line as opposed to a line of Confusion if you do not use your "Sense of Judgement".
Because we have a "Good Nature" our "Good Nature" guides our "Sense of Judgement" in an Upward and Forward straight line. This is why "God" has an Advantage on us.
It is out front or on top and is always looking forward to the Future and "never looks Back". But we humanbeings in the following have Two Obstacles to overcome. Firstly, we must "not look down" or we see (hear) the Shadow; which says, "Do not Judge", which turns you into Confusion and Illusion. Secondly, we must "not look back" or we Stumble over the Shadow and then we wallow in the Mud until we catch sight of God again. Then we must waste (spend) some time cleaning up our Act before we are strong enough again, to think and act in a "Straight Line".

b) So you see folks, to be completely "Free Spirited" is to be with God because It has no Obstacles and can use Its "Sense of Judge ment"and "Good Nature" to the fullest extent. You will note, Proverbs 1, vs (0) says, To be Free is to be Sane, and Sanity has its guidelines, Insanity has no guidelines. This is why the Shadow says, "Do not Judge" because It does not want you to develop any guidelines; So that you might fall into total Confusion and Illusion.

c) God gives us guidelines so that we might develop our "Sense of Judgement" and in turn our "Good Nature". God says, make Decisions and Judgements daily, yes "Judge and be Judged" But in my Fashion; Which is to say, But "Do not Condemn", But rather "Forgive" as you keep going on your way Frontward, showing the alternative.

d) "To Condemn is to Look Back"
To Forgive is to Look Ahead (Frontward)
"To Judge is to Know the Difference"
To Know the Difference is Genius. Genius is a Glimpse of God. "Saint BILL" has a Glimpse of Genius. Ha, Ha, Ha, Ha, Ha,....
I had to laugh. And someone said, I did not have a Sense of Humor. Ha, Ha, Ha.............

Another laugh..
Anyway, Onward with the task at hand.
Which is: To keep Looking Up and walk (Stomp) on the Shadow.

e) Judgement: (has Four stages)
1) Gather the Facts.
2) Weigh them (Pro & Con)
3) Decide (Decision) (Good or Waste)
4) Action (Take Initiative)

(Without Action there is no Judgement, just wish full thinking)

PROVERBS 12

a) It might be said that animals are smarter than Humanbeings. Yes, animals know what to do for life by Instinct. Humanbeings have to be taught almost everything they know.

So what makes it better to be a Humanbeing than to be an Animal. Well the answer is, Humans make progress, Animals do not..

Animals are Perfect, they know everything they need to know, and when you are Perfect you do not make progress.

Humanbeings are like their God, Alive, Active and Good and always changing and improving Its ways and means to meet and win any challenge the Future may bring, and this spells Progress.

b) God says, Life begins at conception. At conception your Soul is born and God prepares a Spot for you in Heaven upon your conception. Now regardless of the weather of your Life your Soul goes to Heaven. This means that if you abort a child or a fetus you will meet him/her in Heaven someday and he/she will say, " You robbed me of a Life on Earth, you Scum. " But you are Forgiven, you Scum".

Shadow says, You are a "Nobody" until you are "born again"; And even then it is only Temporary.

c) God says, Face me, look my way and the Shadow will disappear
Shadow says, Do not look at God, Pleeease.

PROVERBS 13

a)   Profanity is the mark of a conversational cripple.

b)   Someone once said to the Shadow, If you are so smart, Change this Stone into a Loaf of Bread so I can eat; And the Shadow said, No problem, but I am thirsty and drink comes first; So I will change this bottle of water into a bottle of Whiskey,......Zap it is done,... Come, It is true, Believe me, Please, I love you.

c)   A wise person once said, Forget the Shadow's version of Life, those are "the last days" of a Doomsdayer's wishfull thinking of the fruitation of Its wish for Death. God sees no end to Life, only the Future and the Present. (And I say, Yes folks, Life's Soul (Spirit). is Everlasting and we all meet in Heaven to live with God Eternally.

d)   Look forward to the Future and It will come and leave you a beautifull Present..
Look backward to the Past and It will never come but Rob you of the Present you have.

PROVERBS 14

a) Some people grow up to get their head above the Grass. Some people grow up to get their head above the Corn. Some people grow up to get their head above the Maple Trees. Some people grow up to get their head above the Fir Trees. And finally, Some people grow up to get their head above the Redwood Trees in California. (The Tallest in the World)

b) People are lost in the Grass without "The Compass". People are lost in the Corn without "The Compass". People are lost in the Maple Trees without "The Compass". People are lost in the Fir Trees without "The Compass". People are lost in the Redwood Trees without "The Compass". (A certain Someone with his head above the Redwood Trees wrote "The Compass" and Drew a Road map through all the Forests.)

c) Some people do not get above the Grass, so they congregate, "Till" a patch of ground, and claim they now know God.

Excerpt From "Object, MASTERS DEGREE"

Dear Friends and Children of All ages: In the Beginning there were small numbers of People on the Earth. There were Lush Forests and Gardens of Fruit and Vegetables. All lived in Peace and Harmony as there was a Surplus of everything. All Praised God the Real, "The Spirit of Goodness", as they Feared Nothing and they wanted for Nothing, as all their Needs were provided.

Then gradually the population of various regions increased and gradually there became a necessity to Save some Seeds and plant your own Garden.

Of course we know what happened, Some people were to Lazy to do some work and so they started to take from their Neighbours Garden.

Then it became necessary to make some Rules and Regulations to control the Free-Loaders.

The Free-Loaders did not like this, so they got together and formed a Mafia. Yes, organized Crime. The Leader of the first Unit of organized Crime went by the Name of Juda. Juda had a Son called Abraham and so they together wrote out the terms of their Ideology. Their Ideology was called the "Master vs. Slave" Idea.

Otherwise called a Dictatorship. In it, anyone who Joined their Organization was called a "Saint". And all of the Working Society were called "Sinners".

The First Rule that Juda and Abraham made was that they (the Mafia) made all of the Decisions, and all of the "Sinners" were Just their "Slaves" and not allowed to make any Decisions of their own or they would Die.

The Mafia declared themselves God's Children and their Ideology (Theology) the Law of God, and that according to the Law, they could Kill anyone who Disobeyed the First Law. Of course we know One thing lead to another,...and soon "Society as a Whole" (The Workers, The True Saints) had a problem. Yes, How to control "The Mafia". (The Free-Loaders, The Dictators) (The Frauds) Yes, "Society as a Whole" had to get Organized and form a Ideology (Philosophy) of their Own. They decided to call it a "Democracy".

Well, as we know, "Society as a Whole" (Democracy) has survived and thrived. And "Dictatorships" are losing the Battle. And "The Mafia" has been Isolated in a Small area in the Middle East, and surrounded by the Good-Guys (The Police), and "The Mafia" will die a Natural Death as the Old go to heaven, and the Young are Converted to "Previewism", a Philosophy of Freedom of Thought for all and a Philosophy that says, "We are Masters of Our own Destiny".

Yes, We all know that God set us Free in the Beginning and allowed Us to make our own Rules and Regulations to achieve Peace, Harmony, and Equality for All of Humankind throughout the World.

Yes, We are on the Road to Happiness, Decency, Prosperity, and Peace of Mind throughout the World within Three (3) Hundred years, as a Result of God the Real, "The Spirit of Goodness", revealing to "Saint Bill" the words of "THE COMPASS", (A New Bible) (The EverLast Testament) Yes, the True Covenant of God the Real.

Thanks for Listening, as ever in, "The Spirit of Goodness",
"Saint Bill" (Head Coach), A Servant for God's sake.
(Acts 26, v.16-18) (John 7, v.16-18) (1 Jn. 4, v.20) (2 Thes.2, v.9-11)
Previews Institute of Universal Philosophy.
"Thank you, Dear God, Thank you."

PROVERBS 15

a) If, while you are facing your God and your friend is facing the other way, your God says, Your friend is a "Child of the Shadow" because he/she will not face Me:..........What have you learned?.... You have learned that your God is the Shadow. Because you know that the Shadow has not created anyone. God created us All. Therefore, It is a Lie to say you are a "child of the Shadow". And if It Lies your God is the Shadow on every count. So you Look Up and Turn and go with your Friend.

b) Yes, my friends, we have "no children of the Shadow" on Earth, we have only "Children of God". (Most are looking Up most of the time; Some are looking Down; Some of the time; Let us always draw it to their attention in God's fashion.)

PROVERBS 16

a) Quick Death at an old age is a Blessing.
Slow Death at an old age is the Weather.
Quick Death at a young age is the Weather.
Slow Death at a young age is a Blessing.

b) The Escape from Reality, is
The Gateway to Illusion, and/or
The Gateway to Truth and Reality, is
The Escape from Lie and Illusion.

c) A Truth is very Simple and stands on
 Its own.
A Lie is very Complicated and needs many
Crutches.

d) To prove you Love God, you must,
Firstly: Love people (Humanity)
    2) Forgive people (their Shortcomings)
    3) Face Reality (Accept and make the best of what life hands you.)
    4) Count your Blessings.
    5) Remember: You Reap what You Sow, But Manifold.

Thank you, Dear God, Thank you.
B.H., M.A., L.W.
Alias: "Saint BILL"

ACTIONS

Speak Louder than

WORDS

ACTIONS to Promote and Achieve the Objectives.

A Good person follows God, we shall call him/her a Police-person.

A Bad (Wasteful) person follows the Shadow, we shall call him/her a Criminal.

And in between we have Hypocrites saying one thing and doing another.

Ob - 13) **Tolerance**

Ac) To promote Intolerance, you say to your neighbour... "I.. am a child of GOD"... and your neighbour will say,.." who in Hell are you".

To promote Tolerance, you say to your neighbour.. "You...are a child of God"... and your neighbour will say,..."Well, Thank you"..and return the compliment. (If not, then pause.........then say,..."Some people see life through the eyes of the Shadow") (Then leave it at that)

Ac) The worst kind of Intolerance you can show a person is to say to your neighbour..."You are a child of the Shadow",...because that is Hate and a Lie,... You are a child of God, sometimes looking down or back, But always a child of God.

Ob - 4)	<u>Harmony amongst Humankind</u>
Ac.	To achieve harmony among Human kind you follow this simple Rule: "When You speak,...I Listen,... and When I speak,.. You Listen". No interuptions, No contradictions,... Just Listen until I am finished. Your turn will come... AGAIN...soon.

And Remember, The mark of a Fool is when someone swings his/her hand outward and says,... "I do not want to hear it". (So you see only Fools interupt).

Ob -14)	<u>Understanding and Rememberance</u>
Ac	As mentioned in Ch.1, vs. 24-13,... When you worship, celebrate or praise God, do it in a Circle. Also as you know, Proverbs 4, vs. (g) says, "My Summit is my Home and My Home is my Summit" and my congregation is my Family.

Therefore "Saint Bill" suggests you buy a Round Table for your Kitchen. And at each meal you all join hands, Look Up, and say Grace to Our Dear God.

(Recite a short proverb). Then remember   that a chain is only as strong as its weakest link. And also remember,...... that which comes First is Last and that which comes Last is First. Which means, that what the Last one says is just as important as what the First one says,... and vica-versa. (The Understanding will follow)

This Do in Rememberance of "Saint BILL".

Ob - 6)   To distribute the wealth and abundance of God's Food and Essentials of life to the Needy throughout the world.

Ac   Give some to Charity. The Employee (Individual) six (6%) per-cent of your gross income. The Employer (Corporation) twenty (20%) per-cent of the Net, Net Profit.
We realize this sounds a bit High,
but it is better to shoot High than Low.

Ob - 2   To keep people Free of Guilt, Fear, Doubt and Illusion.

Ac	We all know that to Forgive is to Forget. Therefore the Shadow is again, as always, a Fraud, a Hypocrite. It says, You are forgiven (But not Forgotten),... You have to Answer on Judgement Day. (Fraud)
	The first thing that God says to you on Judgement Day is,...."Around here we Look to the Future, Not the Past,... Is that Understood: And you say, "Yes",... And God says, Fine,... Welcome Home, My Child.
Ob - 3	To set in people a frame of mind to achieve the above.
Ac	Read from "The Compass" daily in rotation (Front to Back to Front)
Ob - 15	Enthusiasm
Ac	Think Enthusiastic and you will act Enthusiastic. Act Enthusiastic and you will be Enthusiastic. Be Enthusiastic and you will Feel Enthusiastic. Feel Enthusiastic and you gain Energy. (Oh, Boy!... Am I Enthusiastic!!!)

Ob - 1)   To make and keep people Happy go Lucky

Ac   Face Reality; Accept and make the Best of what life hands you and take advantage of opportunity.

Ob - 5   To bring people to leave this world a better <u>place than when they came into it.</u>

Ac   Read Ch. 1, vs. 23.

Ob - 9)   To Foster and develop among Its' members and the World at large a recognition of the importance of the "Good Natured God" in their life and for they themselves to foster and develop their "Good Nature" as a compliment to Our Dear God.

Ac   Read From the "Compass" daily in rotation.
(Front to Back to Front) and Practice what you Preach. It is simple because it is Reality.

Ob - 12	To Place a copy of "The Compass" in every Home in every Country of the World as soon <u>as possible, by Sale and / or by Gift.</u>
Ac.	Follow the example of Charity and Assumption on the Last page of this "Compass". (Special Life-time Offer)
Ob - 16	In Summary: To Relieve poverty. (Both Physical and Spiritual poverty.)
Ac.	Preach by Letter, by Magazine or by Television, and by http://www.previews-inc.com (As when you Relieve Spiritual poverty, We take Action and Relieve Physical poverty.)

Thank you, Dear God, Thank you.
B.H., M..A., L.W.

THE
COMPASS
Supplement # 2

The Letter of The Truth
The Whole Truth and
Nothing But The Truth
So Help Me God.

by

W.J. (Bill Handel, M.A., L.W.
Alias: "SaintBILL"

Proverbs 17

a) God always has a Clear Conscience because It always Forgives and Hands out Blessings to keep you in Reality and Free to Obey.

Shadow (the Accuser) is saddled with Guilt, Fear, Doubt and Illusion because It always Condemns and Hands out Punishment or threatens to and makes you a Slave to It, to have you pay a Sacrifice.

b) God puts Its Arm around you, and you Look Up, and turn and go to the Right,.... Soon learning to say, Thank you for my Blessings my Dear God.

Shadow says, I am God, please, I love you,.. Look down and watch me,.... and You soon say,... I am confused,... It says, I love you, but hands out nothing but Punishment.

Then the Shadow says, do not worry about it,... Suffering makes you Strong.

And I say, Hog Wash,... Suffering makes you a Sucker for more Suffering,... Which leads to a weak and Sick mind. (Proverbs 5,..vs.(c))

Thank you, Dear God Thank you, for true Insight.
P.S., Have you figured it out yet,.. Well, I will give you a clue,...(The Shadow is a Liar, Remember) (And God speaks with Actions.)

c)   To Judge is to have a Conscience and
To have a Conscience is to Judge.
To have a Clear Conscience is to Forgive.
To have a Guilty Conscience is to Condemn.
To Forgive is to Hand out Blessings.
TO Condemn is to Hand out Punishment.

Proverbs 18

Some people say, You go to Heaven if you believe in the Tradition of "Constant".

Some people say, You go to Heaven if you believe in "Abraham". (Real Character)

Some people say, You go to Heaven if you believe in "Robin Hood". (Fictional Character)

Some people say, You go to Heaven if you believe in "Muhammad". (Real Character)

Some people say, You go to Heaven if you believe in "Buddha". (Real Character)

Some people say, You go to Heaven if you believe in "Singh" (Real Character)

Some people (Previewlites) say, All people go to Heaven because All people Believe in Our Dear God, and Our Dear God Believes in All people. There is no such thing as an "Atheist". That is a Fictional Character. (a Shadow). Yes, You see your Soul (Spirit) belongs to God and therefore "Salvation" is your God Given "Birth-Right".

What we must remember is "You reap what you Sow) on Earth,... And this depends on your
Definition of Good or Waste.,,, And so you know that what is one persons "Good" is sometimes
another persons "Waste". and what is one
persons "Waste" is sometimes another persons "Good".,,,
And we also know, It is a Big, Big
World,... right, right, RIGHT.
Thank you, Dear God, Thank you.

Proverbs 19

a)   In life, Aggression is a Sin against Humanity; Self Defense is an Act of God.

b)   God is Broad and Open Minded.
Shadow is Closed and Narrow Minded.

Proverb 20

a) The Garden of the Shadow has been plowed up. The Shadow Exposed. Its Back broken. And my rubber Rubber Heel has disintegrated the Earthworm to Dust. The Spell is Broken. The Source of the Condemnation is exposed. The Curse is lifted and is no more. Disappeared by the Light of "Our Dear God".

b) Now "Our Dear God" has spoken with Actions from above,... You are Free to Use your Sense of Judgement to fullfill your Good Nature,... You are Forgiven your Misjudgements to keep nullified the Shadows' attempting grip,... And You are Blessed with Life upon life upon Life, as it was in the Beginning, is now, and Ever shall be, World without End.

Thank you Dear Good Thank you

B.H., M.A., L.W.
Alias, "Saint BILL".

Proverb 21

Dear Friends in "Saint BILL",

a) A good analogy just occurred to me, to explain the workings of the Shadow's Theology.

b) It says to you, come to My House of God and it will make you Happy and fulfilled. There are no Doors or Windows so you can Come and go as you please.

c) Now if you are lured to come to the House,..as you approach, Its Helper meets you at the Door and says,..Welcome Home,..Come in and I will show you around. And then he says,.. Watch your step as I take you to the Living room,.. And so you Look down as he takes you down the Hall toward the Living Room,.. After a few corners he says,.. We are here, you can Look up now.

d) Now as you look up, you see nothing but Mirrors,.. Mirrors upon Mirrors. (Illusions upon Illusions),..and you do not know which way to turn and you can not find your way out without his help,...Now he says,.. sorry,.. I can not take you to the Front door unless you Bow down and worship My God,.. So you Bow down,..

Now he says, you are a Sinner, You are Bad,.. I can not take you to the Front door unless you give me a Fee (a Sacrifice), to make it simple, a $100.00 to forgive your Sins,.. So you give him a $100.00,.. You have no choice because you are in a Twisted, Twisted Web, and by now you are convinced that you need to pay God a Sacrifice for your Forgiveness. And furthermore you are convinced that you are a miserable, miserable person,.. And of course you know that misery loves Company. And so you continue to Bow and pay,.. Bow and pay and look for more Company.

e) There is no way out of the Web unless the Helper Trips Up. Yes, you see the Helper is only Human and so he sometimes gets confused too and mistakenly takes you to the Front door and Trips outside,.. Now as you go out with him, you Run for your life, Just Run and never look back because you are so happy that you are Free but can not believe it,.. So you Run and never look back until one day you realize you are actually out and Free.

f) Then you are able again to slow down or relax and again begin to lead a normal life as "Our Dear God" wants it to be. Free from all Illusion, Fear, Doubt or Guilt.

g) Yes, God's Love is Free, God's Forgiveness is Free, God's Understanding is Free, And You are Free to Use your Sense of Judgement to avoid the Pitfalls of life and not have to suffer needlessly.

h) Yes, My Friends, The Shadow says, Do not Judge, (Do not eat of the Fruit of the Tree of the knowledge of Good and Bad) as you have probably heard before. Well, the reason It does not want you to develop your Sense of Judgement is because It does not want you to learn Right fromWrong, Good from Bad, or True from False, and just walk around in circles like a useless imbecile hitting Pitfall after Pitfall.

i) Friends, I am telling you my life's story,.. You are looking at someone who has been there. And so to make a long story short, as I was Running, It occurred to me (my Dear God told me) that I must start Writing down the path to the Front door, before I Forget. So my Friends, I started Writing down every Twist and Turn that is necessary to unravel the Web, so that one can find the Front door.

j) Friends, I say I believe in Multi-culturalism or Freedom of Worship. I do not mind the Muslims, I do not mind the Buddhists, I do not mind the Sikhs, I do not mind the Hindus, and I do not mind the West Indians, the beautiful WestIndians, I say,.. But in my opinion, Lies, Fantasy and Illusions after a Layman and Lies, Fantasy and Illusions after a "Helper" are one and the same thing,.. And that is Shadow Worship. And you know what that means.

k) Yes, there is one exception to Freedom of Religion and that is "Shadow Worship". When they stand there and say,.. they can Kill in the name of God, or on God's Orders,.. I say you poor distorted Shadow Worshipper,.. And when they say, God needs or wants a Sacrifice (Fee) for Forgiveness,.. I say, you poor miserable Shadow Worshipper.

And when they say, that God made a "Deal" with the Shadow to "Share Power",...if the Shadow could convince a Mortal man to (Commit Suicide) stand up and be Killed as a Sacrifice (Fee) to Forgive all our Sins, (Sins that have already been forgiven and forgotten),.. by saying to him,.. You will be Worshipped along with me,...I say, the poor pitiful man and the Dirty Bastard Shadow,..

What a Twisted, Twisted pile of mesh,... All for a Sacrifice that "Our Dear God" does not want or need,.. All for Glory that belongs to "Our Dear God",.. All for Vanity and Waste,...And I say, You poor miserable pitiful Distorted Shadow watchers,...

I) But you are an Illusion,.Shadow, and anything you say is an Illusion,.Shadow,.. So Go and Stay in Hell, "ALONE ",.. Out in Outer Darkness, beyond the reach of Light,.. and stay there. We need you there for Reference.

That about sums it up, eh, My Friends. Thanks for Listening.

W.J. (Bill) Handel, M.A., L.W.
Alias, "Saint BILL".

Note:

M.A.	=	Mentally Alert
L.W.	=	Lead the Way

THE END

THE
BOOK
OF
INSIGHTS

Prophecy Fulfilled
As The Curse is Lifted
And is No More.

By:
W.J. (Bill) Handel, M.A., L.W.
Alias, "Saint BILL"

The "INSIGHTS",

Table of Contents:

Chap. 1	Page 178	Chap. 25, Page
Chap. 2	Page 184	Chap. 26, Page
Chap. 3.	Page 188	Chap. 27, Page
Chap. 4.	Page 195	
Chap. 5.	Page 200	
Chap. 6.	Page 205	
Chap. 7.	Page 210	

INSIGHTS

Chapter 1 Part "A"

1. In life we have Real Characters and we have Fictional Characters. The Real Characters are prone to Truth and Reality, and the Fictional Characters are prone to Lies and Illusions.

2. In life we have God (the Real) and we have God (the Fraud,) the Fictional, the Illusion, yes, The Shadow). And so it seems there are Two Gods, but in fact there is really only One because the other is a Fraud, fictional Illusion.

3. God (the Real) speaks with Actions not with words because Actions speak Louder than words. God (the Fraud) speaks only with words, empty words.

4. Because God (the Real) would not talk to Humankind with words but only with Actions, the Fictional Character (the Shadow), seemed to appear and talked to them, but only with words and no Actions. And so the Lies began; This created a problem, a Fictional Problem, not a Real problem. God (the Real) had no problem. God the Fraud) had a problem; It could not consummate. But it was a Fictional problem, not a Real problem. God (the Real) does not want to consummate, any further than It already has.

5. And so the Fictional Character prepared a Fictional Solution to a Fictional problem. It (the Shadow), by way of counterfeit Miracles, brought forth a man that said He was God. A man that said, he had been to Heaven and had talked to God in person. And that now He had all the answers. But the problem was that He was only Fictional and there where no more answers after than before He supposedly appeared.

6. And so now that we know that God (the Real) has no problems we simply have to go back to the basics and learn to read the Actions of God not the words of the Shadow.

7. We know the Action of God produced an Apple tree. What is God saying; God is saying, I am the provider, Take and Eat. We know the Action of God produced the Sun. What is God saying; God is saying, I want to keep you warm; When God says, I want to keep you warm, what else is It saying; It is saying, I Love you because we know that Love is warm and compassionate. We know that the Actions of God say, I do not keep records, I forget very easily and quickly. What is God saying; God is saying, I forgive you for your shortcomings. We know that the Actions of God produced the Universe and all that is in it and on it. What is God saying; God is saying, I am the creator. We know that the Actions of God produced Everlasting life in Its image.

What is God saying; god is saying, You will be welcome in Heaven, have no doubt; When God says, You will be welcome in Heaven,. What else is It saying;

It is saying, Life is Everlasting, have Faith because God with all Its infinite wisdom and mercy would not have created a Universe and all that is in it and on it and Manifested Itself in the Human mind, without creating a Heaven for us to go to in the hereafter.

8. We know that the Action of God make it untouchable; What is god saying; god is saying, I am a Spirit. We know that the Actions of God are Good and make us Happy. What is God saying; God is saying, I am " The Spirit of Goodness." We know that the Actions of God make It very complex. What is God saying; God is saying, I have many characteristics. When God says, I have many characteristics,. What else is It saying; god is saying, All from the same seed of course, that being the "Good" one. We know that the Actions of God make God real,. What is God saying; god is saying, Be realistic and follow your sense of Reason and Sense of Judgement so that you do not fall into fantasy and Illusion because that creates problems you do not need.

We know that the Actions of God (The Spirit of Goodness) make God Happy; What is God saying,. God is saying, " Look Up" and Have a Happy Day.

                        B.H. M. A. L. W. " Saint BILL"

PART "B"

The Difference between
A Living God and a Dead God (Shadow)

9. God (the real) says, I produced the Apple tree. (And every year more Apples around to prove that God is Living and Well.)

10. God (the real) says, I produced the Cattle. (And every year more Cattle around to prove that God is Living and Well.)

11. God (the real) says, I produced the Flowers. (And every year more Flowers around to prove that God is Living and Well.)

12. God (the real) says, I am a Spirit, and have many Good Characteristics, but do not speak them; Just show them.

13. NOW the Shadow says, I am God, I walked on water. (And who or what is around to prove it. No-one and Nothing. Proof that it is Dead and Gone.)

14. The Shadow says, I am God, I raised the Dead. (And who or what is around to prove it. No-one and Nothing. Proof that It is Dead and Gone.)

15. The Shadow says, I am God, I opened the River so that the Army could walk across. (And who or what is around to prove it. No-one and Nothing. Proof that It is Dead and Gone.

16. The Shadow says, I am God, Believe my miracles, please, I Love you.

17. Yes Folks, God (the real) follows the Laws of Nature and they speak Truth and Reality. God (the fraud) (Shadow) breaks the Laws of Nature and speaks with Lies and Illusion.

PART "C"

18. I have a question for you. But before the question I want to explain how I came to the question.

19. I was told that, once upon a time there was a boy, about five years old, who was told by his mother that his father was not his real father. He was told that he did not have an earthly father, and that he was not a Freak of nature but that he was a very special child of God, not an ordinary child of God like your brothers and sisters will be, but a very special child of God because you were conceived by a spirit. So that you will understand I will say you were conceived by God.

20. As the child grew up It came to believe It was very special, So special that he believed he might never die because he was conceived by God. In fact he came to believe he was God, when he said things like, If you have seen me you have seen the father,. and God and I are One and so on and on.

Now the question,. At what age or at what point in his life did this boy come to realize that he was not God and that he was just a man like everyone else.

Answer: When he was on the gallows charged with insanity, punishable by death. Yes my friends, when this (boy) man realized he was now going to die he realized that he was just a man and not God.

He admitted it to us all when he said, My God, My God, why hast thou forsaken me. Yes, his God had forsaken him, as the "Fraud" always does when the going gets Tough. God, the Real, stays with you all the way. "The Fraud", the Shadow, disappears when the going gets Tough. And then he realized that he had Forsaken his God, and Died completely ALONE.

Poor boy, All because of a Fairy tale, by his Mother, and a very gullable Father.

Chapter 2

1. Some religions hold God out to be a Jealous, Vengeful, Hateful monster which hands out nothing but punishment. Well, It is obvious these people are looking Down into the Darkness.

   We at "PREVIEWS" are looking Up into the light and hold God out to be a sincere, Loving, Forgiving, Understanding "Spirit of Goodness" with many more Good characteristics, that hands out nothing but Blessings, to one and all alike, without qualifications.

   Now we know that to teach a Lie is a Curse. But to teach the Truth is a Blessing. And for one to teach Both is pitiful confusion and Illusion.

   ooooo0ooooo

2. Some people teach that if you do not Hate your brothers and sisters, your wife and family, yes, even your father and mother, you are not following god, and if you do not follow God you can not go to Heaven. (Lk. 14, v. 26).

Well, we at Previews teach that God is a Sincere, Loving, Forgiving, Ever-understanding "Spirit of Goodness" that can not be offended. Therefore God forgives us all our wrong doings everyday and accepts us all into Heaven any and everyday. But we must remember that our fellow Human beings do not always understand and forgive, and so we reap what we sow,. But god loves us always and proves it by giving us all a sense of Judgement to use, so that we learn right from wrong, true from false, and good from bad. Yes, we must learn to Judge one another as God Judges us. (That is to, Provide the alternative, then forgive, not condemn; Bless, not curse; Reward, not punish.)

Yes, my friends, to Judge is to provide the means by which we learn to see ourselves as others see us. Which is a must lest we fall into total confusion and illusion.

oooooOooooo

3. We find that, God says, I am real, and Shadow (Devil) says, I am real. The question is, which one is telling the Truth. Well, we know Shadow (Devil) is a liar; therefore It is a helpless, useless Illusion. God can and does carry on with or without your help. Shadow (Devil) is nothing without your help. That is right, Shadow (Devil) can do nothing without YOU. God hands out Blessings with or without you. Shadow (Devil) hands out Punishment with and by you, But nothing without you. God says, what you sow, you reap, manifold. Therefore take my Blessings and multiply your return, Materially or Spiritually. Follow Lie and Illusion and you hand out punishment and you reap punishment. But remember, It is your own, not god's, because God gave you a Sense of Judgement to use, so that you learn Right from Wrong. So it is your choice what you reap..

oooooOooooo

4. The biggest Lie the Shadow (Devil) ever told is that "It is Real". Wrong, It is Illusion. The biggest Shadow that seems to appear is the Shadow of the Earth. We call It Darkness or Night, and we have believed that It is Real, but like any other Shadow, It is an Illusion; Because there is Light all around and everything operates the same at Night as in the light, because God can see through the Dark. Yes, It has Intelligence that knows no Barriers.

So you see, the Shadow says, It is alright, No-one is looking; But it is a Lie. God is aware. Yes, God is Omnipresent, and although It is always looking forward to the future, It does know what is going on (happening) behind It, and behind you; Because It can see both ways. Yes, God is so far ahead It is coming from behind.

So you see, You reap what you sow in the Dark or in the Light. So do not believe the Shadow (Darkness), It is a Nothing, an Illusion, a Lie and a Liar.

Outer Darkness, beyond the reach of Light, that in my estimation is Real Darkness, but It is Darkness that we never enter into because It is beyond the reach of God; And we stay within the reach of god. Yes, we Border the outer-Limits of god, Hand in Hand.
(See ch. 9, v.17 of the COMPASS)

Chapter 3
Part "A"

a. The Shadow says, that at the end of Life's road there is a Tee intersection. Right goes to Heaven and Left goes to Hell.

b. Now we know that the Shadow is a Liar; So what else does It say? It says, I am God, Follow me and I will take you to Heaven. And then It makes the conditions of approval so difficult that it is impossible to meet them, so everyone fails the test and subsequently everyone would go to hell if the Shadow had Its way.

c. It says, Go and be perfect, and of course every one fails. It is a little confused because It says, Love your enemies, on the one hand, and on the other hand It says, Hate your mother and father. But it suites the Shadow just fine because everyone fails the test.

d. Now as you go along the road you make a mistake and you say, oh my, how am I going to make it; And the Shadow says, do not worry, I forgive you, keep trying, practice makes perfect.

e. Then at the end of the road the Shadow says, sorry you failed,. Left. Then you say, but you said, I forgive you, and the Shadow says,. AH,. Forgiven but not forgotten, You must answer on Judgement day,. Left.,.....Next.,

f. Question: How in life is one supposed to know whether he/she is following the Shadow or following God.

Answer: Remember the meaning of the word God. God means Good and Good is Truth, Love, Forgiveness, Understanding, Tolerance, Enthusiasm, Happiness, Charity, and so on,. And remember that God says, do as I Do, because I speak with actions, as actions speak louder than words. So if you practice these characteristics of god you will do just fine because when God says, forgiven it is already forgotten. And if someone says, I am God,. Run for your life. (And Read from "the COMPASS")

Part "B"

In the Beginning there was "The Spirit of Goodness" (God) and there were the "Frozen Embryos"., And God said, "Let the Light appear"., And the "Frozen Embryos" became Living Beings, which included the Plants, Birds, Fish, Animals, Humanbeings, and All else that God seen was Living and Good; All the "Living Beings" did not know that they Die or that they Live. They just Exist (Existed).

b) Then it came to pass that God wanted to become known to Humanbeings, so that they would come to know that they have Eternal Life with God.

c) So God manifested and said to a Man and Woman together, Take and Eat of the fruit of the tree of the knowledge of Good and Waste, Yes, learn to Judge one another as I Judge you; And you shall become wise and aware of your maker, and you shall then know that you have Eternal Life with God.

d) Then immediately the Shadow seemed to appear and said, Do not eat of the fruit of the tree of the knowledge of Good and Bad or you shall become aware that you die physically. Then the Shadow said to them, It is not worth it, Do not Judge, so that you stay as the other animals around you, please, I love you.

3

e) And the Man and Woman made the correct decision and decided to eat of the fruit of the tree of the knowledge of Good and Waste, because God did not say, Good and Bad, God said, Good and Waste; And they knew immediately that they were Alive for now and forever and they also knew that they would die physically but not Spiritually, and this is what matters, because physical death is just an Illusion, Life is Real and Eternal

f) Then the Man and Woman said, "Well worth it" because what a Joy they had in coming to know that God was with them always and that they could now make progress with their knew found means of knowledge to creativity.

g) And they said, the fear of the unknown, the fear of change, the Illusion, Yes, the Shadow could go to Hell, out to outer darkness beyond the reach of Light, with Its negative, stagnant attitude.

h) Then they started the task of getting other people to look Up instead of Down. (Ha, Ha, Ha, Ha, Ha,)

i) Then God said, God Bless you, Children; God Bless You

    Thank you, Dear God, Thank you
    B.H., M.A., L.W.
    Alias, "Saint BILL"

PART "C"

1. We all agree that there is only One God, and we all agree that we all have a slightly different point of view or interpretation of God. Yes, God speaks with Actions and we all interpret these Actions slightly differently. Your interpretation is inclined to say that my interpretation is wrong and therefore a lie, and my interpretation is inclined to say that your interpretation is wrong and therefore a lie. But the fact is both interpretations are true if we take the time to understand the others point of view.

2. Now we know, we in turn Act according to our individual interpretation. And so, although we all Act differently, we all Act Good in God's eye because God sees us all from our individual points of view and fully understands us and accepts all our actions as Good. (Some rich in Good and some poor in Good)

3. Because we are not God and can not always understand there are a few limitations we put on our freedom. They are that we should not Lie, Steal, Kill, or Overindulge. So you see, we are really quite Free to do our own thing, and like God, we should accept each others Actions as Good and forgive one another if we do not understand.

4. And so you see, Ignorance, Lack of Understanding, Fear of the Unknown, Fear of Change, these are the Culprits, and they are all Illusion, Yes, Shadow. They do not exist except as to the essence of a Shadow.

5. Yes, now we can understand why God Loves us all, because God fully understands us all and is not Offended by any of our Actions but just calls some of them "Waste".

6. Yes, My Children, in all of God's creation there is only Good and Waste. Not Good and Bad,. Just Good and Waste. If you take a Banana, you have the Good inside and the Peel is the Waste. If you take an Orange, you have the Good inside and the Peel is the Waste. And so it is with all of Humankind, when we do something that we habitually call "Bad",. God says, Oh my, what a Waste.

7. And so you see, With a little Understanding, Love and Forgiveness come easy.

PART "D"

When we say that God is Understanding, we are saying that God is Knowledge because Knowledge brings Understanding; And Understanding brings Love and Forgiveness.

Lack of Knowledge spells "Ignorance", and Ignorance spells "A Blind spot" in your psyche.

If your neighbor tries to enlighten this "Blind Spot" with a Lie, he/she fails because a Lie is more Darkness (Blind Spot) and you both stay Ignorant; And you both disagree.

But if your neighbor tries to enlighten this "Blind Spot" with a Truth, he/she will succeed because a Truth is always preceeded by an Action of God and therefore sheds light on the subject, and you say "Oh, I see!!.. You have then gained knowledge and understanding and with it the ability to love and forgive.

Chapter 4
Part "A"

Some people teach that God is a Jealous, Vengeful, Hateful monster that hands out nothing but punishment and does not accept you into Heaven unless you are perfect or have paid a Sacrifice (Bribe). Yes they say that God is an Extortionist and an Accomplice to murder. Worse yet, they say that God committed premeditated murder. Well, it is obvious these people are looking back into an age of Darkness.

Well, we at Previews are in an age of Truth and teach that God is a Sincere, Loving, Forgiving, Everunderstanding " Spirit of Goodness" that can not be Offended,. Therefore It hands out nothing but blessings and accepts us all into Heaven, just as we are. Beautiful, eh, a God you can and would like to please. But we must remember that our fellow Human beings do not always understand and forgive, and so what we sow, we reap, manifold from our neighbors.

This is why God gave us all a sense of Judgement to use, so that we learn right from wrong, true from false and good from bad. Yes, we must learn to Judge one another as God Judges us. (That is to, Provide the alternative, then forgive, not condemn; Bless, not curse; Reward, not punish.

Yes, my friends, to Judge is to provide the means by which we learn to see ourselves as others see us. Which is a must lest we fall into total confusion and illusion.

Part "B"

Dear Friends,. Before God we are All equal. There is no one Nation, there is no one race, there is no one Person that has any preference before God.

There is no one Religion that has any preference before God, Except the ones that say, there is no preference. This is where "Previewism" stands before God.

The Odd one of us has the gall to say that he/she worships the Evil Spirit as though It were real. (the Gall, eh!) Some of us say they worship the Evil Spirit and the Good Spirit together as One. (a bit confused, eh!) Most, near All of us say we worship "the Spirit of Goodness" because we realize the Evil Spirit is just an Illusion, as in Lie, Darkness, Shadow, Ignorance, Blind Spot in your psyche. (a whole lot of Reality, eh!).
God (the Real) (the Spirit of Goodness) pays no attention to what we say, It only pays attention to what we Do,. Yes, Our actions because Actions speak Louder than words; And It has a very positive approach because It understands All our Actions and Adds up All the Good results for you and leaves (forgets) the Waste.
As you know there is always a little Good in All of us and so we All meet God (the Real) in Heaven when we pass on from here because Goodness no matter how small is never wasted before God, because as you know "the first come last and the Last come first".
P.S. Wanting or claiming Preference before God is Evil and Evil is Illusion and Illusion is Ignorance and Ignorance causes Descension, and Descension is not of God.

Part "C"

4

God (The Spirit of Goodness) has One Face and One Face only. By Its actions It says, You are my children, I provide for you, I have given you strengths, I love you, and have set you Free. And I promise you that when your physical life is over here on Earth, Your Spirit (Soul) shall not die, but meet me (God) in heaven to live Eternally with God in Heaven. Have that Faith and It will bring you Fulfillment.

oooooOooooo

The Shadow has Two Faces and sometimes many more. From one side of Its Face It says, You are Bad, I disown you, You are All condemned to Death, Yes, Fire and Brimstone in Hell.

Then From the other side of Its face, It says, However, If you will pay me a Thousand Dollars ($1,000.00) or maybe even more, I will make arrangements to Forgive you All your Sins, For Life, and you will Live with me in Heaven Eternally. I guarantee it.

(Then an Hour after Its Servant has certified your cheque) The Shadow says, sorry, I made a mistake in my calculations, and I have to Remind you that you are Still condemned to Death. However if you will pay me $2,000.00 or maybe even more, I will make arrangements to Forgive you All your Sins, For Life, and you will Live with me in Heaven Eternally. I guarantee it. etc. etc. I am doing this for you because I Love you., so you owe me,. etc. etc.

P.S.: " Saint Bill" says, Extortion, The Dirty Bastard, no wonder It is alone in Hell.

Part "D"

God is All White, (Knowledge, Light, Goodness) Real. (Action with words)

Shadow is All Black, (Ignorance, Darkness, Bad) Illusion. (Words Only)

Human beings are Grey, (a slightly different mixture for each of us, but Grey.)

So in fact there are only Two entities. (God and Humans)
ooooo0ooooo

God says,. do this, it is Good for you, and I will give you many Blessings.

We find God speaks Truth on every count.

The Shadow says, I am God,. do this, it is Good for you, and I will give you many Blessings.

However, we find the Shadow is a Liar on every count.

It is not God, It is not Good for you, and It hands out punishment with, by and through your neighbor.

But It looses the Game everytime if you Understand and forgive the Ignorance of it all. Yes, we must see through the Scheme of the Shadow, which is to play Ignorance against Ignorance; And then Laughs as we punish ourselves.

This is why we need a Sense of Judgement.

Part " E "

" Our Dear God " (The Spirit of Goodness),
is the opposite of The Shadow (Devil).

	God	**Shadow**
1)	Good	Bad
2)	Happy	Sad
3)	Love	Hate
4)	Courage	Fear
5)	Confidence	Jealousy
6)	Trusting	Jealous
7)	Truth	Lie
8)	Forgive	Condemn
9)	Bless	Curse
10)	Reward	Punish
11)	Understanding	Narrow Minded
12)	Initiative	Procrastination
13)	Judge	Procrastinate
14)	Judgement	Wishfull Thinking
15)	Knowledge	Ignorance
16)	Light	Darkness
17)	Real	Illusion
18)	Reality	Fantasy
19)	Possible	Impossible
20)	Equality	Preference
21)	Rich	Poor
22)	Charity	Greed
23)	Harmony	Descension
24)	Wheat	Chaff
25)	Banana Pie	The Peel
26)	Orange Juice	The Peel
27)	Good	Waste

B.H., M.A., L.W. "Saint BILL"

Chapter 5
Part "A"

The First four Words that comes up, when Disaster strikes are:
> " Dear God, Help me."

1. Dear Friends,. God set us Free to "Reap what we Sow" and hopes we come out a winner. But sometimes we Sow the Good that God gives us and reap (Waste). An example that comes to mind is,. If you plant a kernel of Wheat in a Thistle field, when you harvest and try to make flour you will have Thistle flour not Wheat flour; And it will probably taste Sour or Bitter.

2. But God always stands by to help and bring up the Rear when disaster strikes. The Shadow (Illusions) laugh in our face and leave the Scene, nowhere to be seen again until the Sun shines again.

3. This is why God gave us a Sense of Judgement to use to avoid the Pitfalls of Life. Yes, you see, Illusions are a part of Life, but if we use our Sense of Judgement we learn to decipher Reality from Illusion and avoid the Pitfall of the Illusion.

4. Friends, we know that God is Knowledge, and God knows we are born without it, and so we have lots of Illusions to overcome.

Now we know that before the Judge downtown, ignorance is no excuse; But before God, ignorance is excusable and forgivable, because Ignorance in itself is not Evil or Bad. It is just waste with a lot of "good" potential if we look at Life from a positive point of view; And we know that Forgiveness is positive just like Love, Understanding, and Truth, etc.....

5. So you see, we are all meant to be in the front line, and like God, we have to face the wind and weather as it comes. But we can thank God that It always has a multitude of Helpers standing behind us when disaster strikes, because the Illusions (Shadows) disappear.

6. So my friends, keep up the Good work and do not worry about disaster, as it is never as distasteful as it might seem; and besides it is only temporary.

oooooOooooo

Part "B"

Dear Friends,. We at "Previews" want the World to know the Truth about God.

Yes,   God Loves us,. It never Fears us.
        God Forgives us,. It never Condemns   us.
        God Blesses us,. It never Curses us.
        God Rewards us,. It never Punishes us.

Yes, God is too Smart to be Evil

But we Humanbeings are "a little slow" and do not always catch on to our neighbor's motives. We think he/she is doing something Bad, so we think we have to strike back; And so a vicious circle is started.

However if we asked some questions we would come to understand that our neighbor has Good intentions, and subsequently we would Forgive instead of Condemn, Reward instead of Punish, Yes, Bless, not Curse.

We find that the first way (the Good way) is as a result of Knowledge. The second way (the Bad way) is as a result of Ignorance. Yes you see, Ignorance causes the problem because It allows Illusions in, and Illusion is what we call The Shadow.

Now we can understand why God can always Forgive us, because It knows we are a little slow, ignorant, under an illusion, misled, and not responsible.

So the Object of Life is to get Smart, so that you learn to Understand, Forgive, and Love; And subsequently this brings you Joy, Happiness and Peace of Mind.

ooooo0ooooo

Part "C"

1) Dear Friends,. We at "Previews" are so Glad that " Our Dear God" is a Push-Over. Yes, It loves us and forgives us All our wrong-doings, and just keeps on handing out Blessings; But if we think we can push God around, we are wrong, because when we try to push God around, we are pushing our neighbor around and he/she pushes back. This means we are asking for trouble and ultimately Punishing each other or ourselves.

2) However, if we try to Please God we are pleasing our neighbor and our neighbor returns the favor. And so we are pleasing each other or ourselves and God together, and God just keeps on handing out Blessings.

3) Yes, you see God set us Free in the beginning to "Reap what we Sow" and gave us a choice to look Up and Forward to follow God or look Down and Back to follow the Shadow of God.

4) But we know the Shadow is a Lie, a Fraud, an Illusion, a Nothing and a total Waste. This is why God sees no Bad in us, only Good and some waste; And this is why God can forgive us, because God knows that when we do things we normally call "Bad", God knows we are looking at the Shadow, and the Shadow is just Waste and produces Waste, better known as Punishment, with and by misled people.

5) God looks at you like a Banana or an Orange, you have the Good inside and the Peel is the Waste. so God just discards, leaves, forgets, forgives the Waste because it is behind you and carries you on to a wonderful Future, of course ahead of you.

6) Is this not wonderful that we have such a Beautiful God, always Understanding, Loving, Forgiving and of course Generous,. Physically, Materially and Spiritually.

7) We all know and agree that we are supposed to be just like "Our Dear God", nothing more, nothing less. Yes, this will eliminate the Sorrow and leave you with Happiness and the ability to enjoy your Blessings.

8) Friends, Our generation and our future generations desperately need our message to reach them, to free them of Guilt, Fear, Doubt and Illusion. Please join us today in our efforts to achieve this.

Thank you for your Confidence and Help in our Objectives. Yours Truly, as ever in, "The Spirit of Goodness",

B.H., M.A., L.W.
Alias, "Saint BILL".

Chapter 6   Part A

Dear Friends,. Teach your children to Love their family and friends with all their Heart, but not their Soul, because their Soul belongs to God.

In other words, Love your neighbor but do not worship him/her. Yes worship comes from the Soul and therefore Worship belongs to God.

Because God is infallible, while Humans are fallible. Yes, even the great ones among us are fallible... The Greatest, Mohammed Ali, Fallible. The King, Elvis, Fallible. The Great one, Gretzke, Fallible. All the Great Prophets of old, All Fallible.

As a example I refer to the one that said, Quote, " If anyone comes to me and does not Hate his brothers and sisters, his wife and family, yes, even his father and mother, He can not be my Disciple."

Now we know that any Good and Honest man never asks anyone to do something that he does not do himself. Therefore, we can assume this man hated his mother and father and brothers and sisters,. or preached a double standard.

Furthermore, we know that, If someone says, I love God, and hates his brother, He is a Liar. And we know Liars are Fallible. (1 jn. 4,v.20)

Part B (The Free Spirit)

The Free Spirit thinks front ward, backward, upward, downward, left, right, and every which way.

Yes the Free Spirit is constantly mutating. The mutations in the thought process can be either Realistic or Illusionary. Therefore you have to use your sense of Judgement to stay Realistic or you fall into illusion and confusion.

Therefore the Free Spirit can be either creative and productive or just plain wasteful,. depending on your sense of Judgement.

It all starts with Light entering your Eye. You see something right side up, That is Real. Your Free Spirit turns it up side down, that is Illusion. Secondly, your neighbor describes a Car right side up,. That is Truth, and keeps you in Reality. Then your neighbor describes a Car up side down,. That is Lie, and creates an Illusion in your mind. And we know we can all do without Illusion.

So you see, this is why God sees no Evil (Bad) in us, because God knows we are born a (Green Apple) ignorant, sour, waste, but none the less an Apple with all the ingredients to become Delicious with a little bit of Light (knowledge).

And so we must remember The Shadow is Illusion, and does not exist except as a figment of your imagination. God is Real and knows you are coming to God every step of the way.

6

God knows this and does not pay any attention to Illusion (The Shadow). God just lets time take its course knowing you will quickly develop your sense of Judgement and in turn your Good Nature.

But you must stay Positive, Yes, keep Looking Up to God, not down to The Shadow.

Part C

God is Ever Understanding, Forgiving, Loving, and Real; And hands out Blessings.

The Shadow is Narrow-minded, Vengeful, Jealous, and a Fraud. (A total Liar).)

Humanbeings are caught in the middle sometimes misled by the Fraud (Illusion), which says, I am God, do it this way and I will give you many Blessings; and then Humanbeings, not understanding the negative results of each others Actions, strike at each other with Punishment, and the Shadow just laugh away, saying, God punishes,. (Which is another Illusion) And when you tell someone, It is another Lie,. God is Ever Understanding and Forgives, and hands out nothing but Blessings. So you see, The Object of Life is to follow God's Example. And the Shadow will be left Crying in Its Beer.

Part D

Dear Friends,. If someone should ever say to you, You have a Bad (Sinful) Nature, You just say, Hog Wash,. I was created in the image of God, and God is Good. Therefore I have a Good Nature. I was born Innocent and my God forgives,. Therefore, I stay Innocent with my Good Nature intact.

So you just take your Guilt Trip and get behind me.

Yes Folks, we were all born with a Good Nature inherently. And any story to the contrary is just an Evil Guilt Trip (Lie) as a result of Illusion (the Shadow) trying to gain your Allegiance and then your Sacrifices (Extortion).

This is all serving the Shadow (Illusions) because God (the Real) does not want your Sacrifice,. God wants Obedience; And when God does not get it sometimes, God says, Forgiven,. Now carry on and do it better next time.

That is right Folks, No Guilt Trips from God.
Guilt Trips come from the Shadow (the Sum total of Illusions)

So just remember, In God's eye you are Innocent and have a Good Nature in the likeness of God.

God Bless you as you HAVE A HAPPY DAY!

Part E

Dear Friends,. In God's world you Reap only Blessings, because God always understands and forgives.

In Humankind's world you "Reap what you Sow" because Humans do not always understand and forgive.

Which means that "You Reap what you Sow" is yet another Handy Expression made by Humans and Attributed to God.

God seeds only Good and Reaps only Good. Humans are to Reap the Good they seed, and ask their neighbor to Forgive them the Bad, and in this way not let the Bad come to Fruitation; And then do for others as you want them to do for you, without having to be asked.

Yes, God's Law is "Look Up and Forgive one another and Reap only Blessings." Barring the Weather, of course.

But we must remember, we are only Human, and in exceptional Extreme Cases, " You Reap what you Sow" comes in Handy.

B.H., M.A., L.W. (Alias: " SAINT Bill")

Chapter 7

Part "A"

Dear Friends,. In the Religious circle there are Old Text Books that teach that God condemned us to Death. Well it is obvious that the Authors of these Books were first of all, Negative, then faithless, hopeless, wallowing in Self-Pity, a bit confused, and looking back into Darkness (the Shadow, as It said, I am God); And then to make matters worse they took the next step and became Extortionists.

Well, at Previews, Truth has prevailed in "The COMPASS. The New Text Book of the Future, as it teaches that God always Forgives. It never Condemns because God knew that as It would create Heaven and Earth and Life, being Eternal, there would be a few Chips and Wastes fall by the wayside. God also knew that we would have trouble dealing with, copeing with, and overcoming (avoiding) the unfulfilling influence of the Chips and Wastes (the Shadow).

But God said, Nothing ventured, nothing gained; And so God proceeded with Its Plan of preparing a Spot for each and every one of us in Heaven, that big big outermost circle around our magnificent God. That is right Folks, Our Spiritual life (Soul) lives Eternally with God. That is Reality, because Physical death is just an Illusion and nothing to fuss about.

Now friends, you can see which Text is based on Truth and Reality, and which is based on Lie and Illusion; And it is easy to choose which God you want as your own, because truth is always an obvious and easy choice.
God Bless you as you HAVE A HAPPY DAY!

(And The Glory be to God) Sincerely "SAINT BILL"

Part "B"

Dear Friends,. God (Soul) that lives within you is Born when you are conceived; And It is asleep until you are born into this World; Then It is Awake and begins to learn how to Deal with the Unfulfilling influence of the Shadow (Illusion).

The First step in the Right Direction is when It hears the word "Good". yes, Good Baby. The Second step is when It is told that "Good" is God (soul) within you Expressed.

The third step is when Baby is told that God (Soul) is Real and Eternal. Yes, It lives within you and Never dies but lives eternally with God (Soul) The Spirit of Goodness) in Heaven.

The fourth step is when Baby is told that God (Soul) has many Characteristics beginning with Sincerity (Honesty) (Truth) (Reality), and Curiosity (Questions), and Enthusiasm, perserverance, Love, Forgiveness, Tolerance, Being Lucky, etc. etc.

The Tenth step is when Baby is told that the Mind (has) brings forth many Mutations in Its Thinking and that you have to develop your "Sense of Judgement" so that you can tell, Right from Wrong; Good from Bad; True from False: Reality from Illusion; Possible from Impossible; Productive from Wasteful; Something from Nothing; The Spirit of Goodness from The Shadow.

The Twentieth step is when It is told how to Deal with the Illusion of Physical death. Yes, Baby, you are Alive in Spirit and you Never die in Spirit, but Go immediately to meet your Maker in Heaven; And Physical Death is just an Illusion trying to Distract you from the Reality of Life Eternal.

The Twenty First step is when Baby is told that We are Masters of our Own Destiny. Yes, a person with Goals and Plans becomes Master of his/her own Destiny

A person who Relies on God in Heaven to Reveal his/her Destiny is like a Ship without a Sail,. Because they forget that God set them Free to Drift or Decide on a Direction.

Friends, the above Insight is as a result of Understanding The COMPASS, and is but one page. The COMPASS has over 200 such pages. A must to read and live by.

We look forward to hearing from you, now that you have read The COMPASS, as we are quite confident that you will want to help us get these Concepts (Realities) to the Forefront of Society.

Thanks for Listening,. Yours truly,
As ever in, "The Spirit of Goodness"

Previews Institute of Universal Philosophy
B.H., M.A., L.W. Alias: "Saint Bill"

God Bless you as you HAVE A HAPPY DAY!
(And the Glory be to God)

Part "C"

Dear Friends,. It is evident in many instances that God has a sense of Humor. Take for example the Fictional story that Abraham wrote about Adam and Eve. In it Adam is talking to God and God says to Adam,. You have been Bad, You have disobeyed me.,. I am going to have to Kill you,. Yes, I have to condemn you to Death.

Then Adam says, please God do not do that, please,. Then God says, well alright, I will reduce the Sentence,. I will just put you to sleep for a while. Then Adam says to God, gosh thank you, thank you,. But for how long? And God says, Until Hell freezes over,. But we will not say it that way,. We will say, Until the Graves open up, and we will call that "The Day of Resurrection" (Really a cold day in Hell).

Then God says, to Adam, Now I could Forgive you and let you live, but that is not my Nature, I like to Kill, ah, pardon me, Put people to Sleep.

It is obvious that Abraham was a bit confused and describing God (the Fraud) not God (the Real). The nature of God (the Real) is to Forgive and let the Spirit of God that lives within you continue to live with God in Heaven.

Now Abraham goes on to say that God said to Adam,. If you will have your sons go and Kill your good obedient Brother Robin,. I will Forgive you and you will never die, not even physically. (wow,eh!)

It is obvious that Abraham was really confused and misled. Because God (the Real) says, Thou shall Not Kill,. So use your sense of Judgement and Trust in God's good Judgement and accept that physical death is just an Illusion trying to distract you from the Reality of Life Eternal. Yes, folks, the Spirit of God within you can never die but goes immediately to meet God in Heaven when your Body ceases to function.

This is the way God planned it,. Life in the Womb, Life on Earth and Life in Heaven,. Have faith in this and it will bring you to fulfillment and contentment, as you learn to accept life as it is, Spiritually Eternal.

Part "D"

Dear Friends,. If God had a choice to be Tolerant or Intolerant, what would It be?,. It would be Tolerant.

If God had a choice to Love or to Hate, what would It do?,. It would Love. If God had a choice to Forgive or to condemn, what would It do?,. It would Forgive.

Therefore, If someone says to you God loves you,. That is the Truth. And If someone says to you that God hates you,. That is a Lie. Furthermore, If someone says to you, God forgives you,. That is the Truth. And if someone says to you that God condemns you,. That is a Lie.

Therefore, when Abraham wrote that God condemned Adam and Eve to death,. That was a Lie. God is the same Yesterday, Today, and Tomorrow, therefore God forgave Adam and Eve for any mistakes they may have made in their lives just as It does today; And the Spirit of God that lived within the first man and woman went to Heaven just as the Spirit of God that lives within us does today.

Yes Folks, physical death is just an Illusion trying to distract us from the Reality of Life Eternal. The Spirit of God that lives within each and everyone of us can never die, just as God can never die, but goes immediately to live with God in Heaven eternally when our Body ceases to function.

Just as we do not fully understand the beginning of Heaven, Earth, and Life, so we do not fully understand the tomorrow of Life; But we have the today, and we know that the Spirit of God lives in Heaven and within us and we know that It is Eternal. Yes, once conceived there is no looking back.

We know that the Wisdom of God has no limits and knows no barriers and knows that if we have faith in Eternal life, we will live life to the fullest, both now and tomorrow.

Thanks for Listening, Yours truly,
as ever in, " The Spirit of Goodness"

Previews Institute of Universal Philosophy

B.H., M.A., L.W., ALIAS " SAINT BILL"

Part "E"

Dear Friend,. Are you the type of Individual first in line to help improve our Nation's psychology? If so, you will be interested in becoming one of our <u>Active</u> members.

As you know a lot of us do not appreciate the Ground Swell of Religion in Society that carries us through our life. A lot of us say we do not belong to a Religion, but we forget that Society is in Itself a Religion.

Because we live in a Multi-Cultural Society (Country) we are fortunate to be able to take the (Good) of each Religion and become closer to God than the Individual Religion. In other words, the sum total of all the Parts is greater than any of the Parts. (This is what "Previewism" is all about.)

We do not say, I, I, "I" am a child of God, and get the response of, "Who in Hell are you"., We say, "You" are a child of God, and get the response of, "Well, Thank you, and so are you, Joy to the World."

Friends, the above insight is as a result of Understanding The COMPASS and is but one page. The COMPASS has over 200 such pages. A must to read and live by. Order a Copy for a Friend, today. Only $39.95, but subject to change.

We look forward to hearing from you, as we are quite confident that you will want to help us get these concepts (Attitudes) to the Forefront of Society.

Thanks for Listening,. Yours truly
as ever in, "The Spirit of Goodness"

Previews Institute of Universal Philosophy
B.H., M.A., L.W. ALIAS "SAINT Bill"

God Bless you as you HAVE A HAPPY DAY!
(And the Glory be to God)

THE
BOOK
OF
FURTHERMORES

We have Herein
The Birth of Reality
and
The Death of Illusion

By:

W.J. (Bill) Handel, M.A., L.W.,

Alias: "Saint Bill"

Furthermores

Chapter 1 Part "A"

1) Abraham had a God, It was His Father and his name was Juda. (Result: Judaism) St. Paul had a God, It was His Son and his name was Robin. (Result: Hoodianity).

   Abraham's Father was a Good man,. St. Paul's Son was a Bad man. Both Abraham and St. Paul worshipped their human Idols.

   And God (the Real) The Holy Spirit got Second Fiddle and turned Grey.

2) "St. Bill" has a God, It is neither his Father or His Mother, nor His Son or his Daughter, nor his Brother or his Sister, nor anyone else on this Earth.

   It is The Holy Spirit, redefined as, "The Spirit of Goodness" and It is pure White; And It will stay pure White because It does not have any Human names attached to It, nor any Human connotations.

3) "St. Bill" says, Dear is My God's name, Yes, My God's name is Dear to me. "The Spirit of Goodness" (God, the Real) revealed to "St. Bill" that because God is always looking Forward to the Future and never looks Back, The Philosophy of God, the Real "the Spirit of Goodness" shall be called 'PREVIEWISM" in recognition of the life long Love of the PREVIEWS that Our Dear God gives us.

   oooooOooooo

4) Human Idols are like The Shadow,. They are always around with their Hand Out when the Sun shines,. But when the Clouds come and the Rain falls, (the times of need), they Disappear, no where to be seen, until the Sun Shines again.

5) "The Spirit of Goodness" with all Its Good Characteristics makes you Strong and Flexible, Like a "Steel Glass Ball", and when the Clouds come and the Rain Falls, you are like a Duck, The water just rolls off and leaves you Unaffected; As you realize the Sun is still Shining above the Clouds.

6) So do not worship me, Worship God, (the Spirit of goodness) as the Good characteristics that we learn to use, belong to God, not to me.

Part "B"

SMALL TALK

PREVIEWISM
PREVIEWISM
PREVIEWISM

7) At Previews we believe that the Praise and Glory for the Blessing of PREVIEWISM Goes to Our Dear God.

8) The reason that we should remember the Founder of the Philosophy of PREVIEWISM is to remind us that It is not Flawless.

9) Anyone who claims that his/her philosophy on Earth is Flawless is a Liar and a Thief, trying to rob God of the Glory of Flawlessness.

10) When we meet God in Heaven then we will see Flawlessness; But until then we are trying to look through the Clouds.

11) PREVIEWISM, although not Flawless is the winning combination of Philosophies because It is based on the Actions of God, not the empty words of the Shadow. Yes, Actions speak louder than words. This translates into Truth and Reality, not Lie and Illusion. Yes, Reality is God and God is Reality, Not Fantasy.

12) If you want to Understand Humanity, Life,and God and receive the Joy, Happiness, and Peace of Mind that comes with it, study the Philosophy of PREVIEWISM as manifested in and by The COMPASS. (You will be a Winner in God's eye.)

Part "C"

13) Our second commandment is: Remember that with Life on Earth when we pit the Shadow against God, God always gets the Last word; And the Last word is, FORGIVEN. Yes folks, God keeps all of Its children. It has not lost one yet and never will.

14) Yes Folks, the Condemnation,the Curse, the Shadow's wish for Spiritual death for us has been Nullified and removed, because " Our

Dear God" is Ever Understanding, EverLoving, and EverForgiving; And can not be Offended or Alienated by anyone or anything. yes, God can not be Led or Driven to retaliate. (no Consequences) Consequences come from Humanbeings as a result of Ignorance which allows you to Act on Illusion instead of Reality. God understands this and so always says FORGIVEN.

Part "D"

15) And so today I hand each and everyone of you a Bushel of Mustard Seed. (The COMPASS) As you plant one seed in yourFriend's mind, It will grow a Bushel of Mustard Seed. Then He/She will begin to plant. And if each of you will get rid of just Half a Bushel in your life time we will see "Our Dear God's" Kingdom reign the World over before My 300th birthday. (I challenge you to say, "Let's Do It".

Chapter 2   **Part "A"**

1) In life we come to Realize that "Our Dear God" is EverUnderstanding, Loving, and Forgiving; And when we see a Breathless, Still body, We have a choice.

2) We can say, God killed him/her, or we can say, God invited him/her to come to Heaven.

3) The First choice leaves us Faithless, Hopeless, Wallowing in Self-Pity, and Feeling accursed. (That is following Lie and Illusion)

4) The second choice gives us Joy, Happiness, and Peace of mind and fills us with Hope, Faith, and Charity. (This is the way to live successfully; How do I know, "The COMPASS" tells me so) (Yes, God always hands out Blessings) (If it did otherwise, It would not be God anymore) (This is following Truth & Reality)

Part "B"

5) Dear Friends,. When we Believe in Life Eternal, we Believe in "The Spirit of Goodness' (God, the Real) because God, the Real (The Spirit of Goodness) does not Die in any way, shape or form.

6) When we Believe that Death is Final, we Believe in The Shadow, (Illusion) because The Shadow does not Believe in God (Life Eternal),. Remember, The Shadow is a Liar.

It says, I am God, but it knows It is Lieing. It says, Follow me and I will take you to Heaven, and Then The Shadow says, Death is Final. (A Liar on every count.)

7) And so you see Our Dear God gives us a choice,. We can choose to Believe in Life in heaven and Live in Heaven on Earth as a Result. Or we can choose to Believe in Death as Final, and Live in Hell on Earth as a Result.

8) But regardless of which you choose to Believe, when your Body ceases to function, You will wake up to Life in Heaven quite different from what you Did or Did not expect. (See Compass, Ch. 5, v.-10-16) (So you see, Despite yourself, You are going to Heaven) (Because God is God, not The Shadow).

Part "C"

1) Dear Friends,. 6000 years ago, Abraham's Father said, "I am God", and Abraham's Father said to Abraham,. If you will Kill your Son, you will prove that you Love me more, and then I will give you the Keys to the Lock on Heaven's door.

2) It is obvious Abraham's Father was following the Shadow because we know that God (the Real) does not Tempt us to Kill. God tempts us to Procreate and Love.

3) 2000 years ago St. Paul's Son said, "I am God", I can walk on water, I can raise the Dead, I can change a Bottle of Water into a Bottle of Whiskey by snapping my Finger., I can move a Mountain by saying Mountain move.

4) It is obvious that St. Paul's Son was a Liar and a Dreamer (The Shadow)

5) Now St. Paul's Son said to St. Paul,. If you will "Write" that I personally Rose from the Dead and Floated up into the Clouds, I will give you the Keys to the Lock on Heaven's Door.

6) It is obvious St. Paul was a bit confused and very Gullable.

7) 1600 years ago Mohammed said, I am a descendant of the first man and woman. "I am Not God", but I understand what these people are talking about. Here in my Book I have explained it all in the Right Light. Take It and Follow me.

8) It is obvious this Honorable Man tried his best to make Something out of Nothing.

9) 8 years ago, when I was 51 years old, I, "St. Bill" was looking for a Sign from God to tell me to start writing. Well, as I previously said, I started writing when I stopped Running and 3 years later, I was looking through an old Scrap book of Pictures,. And I found the Sign that convinced me, that I was on the Right Track.

It was a Picture of a Circular Star, hovering over my Right Shoulder. (A Light in the Night), and of course my beautiful Wife. Yes, the Sign said, "A Friend in Need is A Friend in Deed". Yes folks, I realized I was on the Right Track when I realized that God Speaks with Actions not with Words. Yes, Actions speak Louder than Words. Yes, when we learn to Read the Actions of God, which comes by Seeing the Results of God,. Then we realize that God is "The Spirit of Goodness", and the first Characteristic of (The Spirit of Goodness) is Sincerity, (Truth) (Honesty). Yes, God has The Spirit of Truth and Reality,. Not Lie and Illusion, (Fantasy); And when you look to The God of Reality (Actions), rather than the Empty words of the Shadow, You will find that "Help" comes from The Spirit of God within you,. Not from a Human Shadow.

10) Now let us get back to the keys to the Lock on heaven's door. Well Folks, as you have already guessed, there are No Keys. The Door is Swinging both ways on Its hinges; And on the Floor on the Right hand side there Lays an Open "Combination Lock" (The Compass), and the Combination Number is ISBN-0-9697487-0-1,. You will find it on the Back cover of "The Compass". It is there for you in case someone Closes the Lock (The Compass).....Funny, Funny, eh! Ha, Ha, Ha, Ha,. "But How True".

11) And so in conclusion I say, "I am Not God",. I would be a "Shadow Damned" Fool if I did. God is God is "The Spirit of Goodness", The Spirit of Truth and Reality,. And the Reality is that The Spirit of God Lives within Us and can not Die, but goes to Live Eternally with God in Heaven when our Body ceases to function. So, follow God, the Real, " The Spirit of Goodness",. Not God, the Fraud, " The Shadow",

P.S.: You will be given a Copy of the Picture at my Funeral Celebration. My only Hope is that Someone finds a way to preserve It indefinitely. Because it is Beautiful and Superb. I was 26 years old at the time and my wife was 24.

Thanks for listening, Yours truly,
As ever in, " The Spirit of Goodness"

B.H., M.A., L.W. Alias, "Saint Bill"

Chapter 3   Part "A"

1. The Previewlite knows, without a doubt, for certain, that he/she is going to Heaven, because God, the real, "The Spirit of Goodness" says, All my Children, Yellow, Red, Black, White, and Brown, throughout the world, will meet me in Heaven; The Rich, the Poor, the Good and the Seemingly Bad, all belong to me. Yes, All my Children will meet me in Heaven.

2. The Shadow Worshipper is Hoping upon Hope, Wishing upon Wish that he/she is going to Heaven, because The Shadow says, Follow me and I will take you to Heaven,. And then says, Ah!. Not all who come to me and say, God, God, will be accepted into Heaven,. No, Not all,. Only those who have done my Will. (And of course No One has done Its Will,. Be Perfect,. So Everyone goes to Hell according to The Shadow.) (St. Bill, says, Balderdash, to that Earthworm)

Part "B"

1. God, the real, "The Spirit of Goodness" Loves each and every one of us on Earth, Individually, Just as we are,. So much that It calls each and every one of us a "Saint". Is that not wonderful, Yeh!!, that is wonderful.

2. And the "Shadow Damned" Shadow says, we are a "Nobody". (No wonder we say, To Hell with you, You worm)

Part "C"

1. The Shadow (Illusion) says, God Cursed you,. and now you are pre-occupied by the prospect (possibilities) of the Curse,. So now you will live in constant Fear of God.

2. Then The Shadow says, If you will Bow Down and Worship me, I will Lift the Curse off your mind and you will be Free again.

3. So you Bow Down and Worship, and The Shadow says, Just stay there,. Ahh, you make me feel so great when you so feed my Ego; I will get around to Lifting the Curse Tomorrow. (Of course we know tomorrow never comes)

4. The Fact is, God does not Curse, It only Blesses us. The Shadow lied, and as you know The Shadow lies on every count.

5. The second Fact is, You do not need the Shadow to Lift the Curse; Remember, It is the Shadow's Curse and It (the Curse) has no power,. If you turn and Look up to God, the real. Yes, God, the real, says Open your Eyes and you will find you are in Reality, and The Reality is, You are Free to receive God's Blessings on Earth and in Heaven at all times, and most harm that comes your way, you bring upon yourselves, as you occasionally look down or back; The remainder is as a result of the weather, because as you can See, I Love, Forgive, Bless and Reward; Not Fear and Hate, Condemn, Curse or Punish. (Yes, there is No longer any Curse,. Rev. 22,v.3)

Part "D"

1. Dear Friends,. To Love and Forgive is of God, and To Hate and Condemn is of The Shadow. To be Positive is of God. To be Negative is of The Shadow. To look Forward to the Future is of God. To look Back to the Past is of The Shadow. To have Applied Faith, based on Actions, is of God. To have Blind Faith, based on Words only, is of the Shadow.

2. By Nature we Procreate and Love to produce life and life is of The Spirit of God. (Life in the Womb).

3. By Nature we have Labor pains to produce life on Earth, and life on Earth is of God if we look up and forward to God,. And Not down or back to the Shadow.

4. By Nature our Body ceases to function to produce life in Heaven. Yes, when our Body ceases to function it is the Means by which God Free's our Spirit (Soul), So that It can go Home to God in Heaven. yes, God loves Company,. And God gets the Company because It is always positive and Enthusiastic and an Excellent Host. Always looking forward to the Future.

5. Yes, very Strong and Steadfast, Inspiring Serenity to accept the things we can not Change, and Courage to Change the things we can, and the Wisdom to know the Difference.

6. Yes, God says, Judge and be Judged to make progress, but in My fashion, which is to provide the Alternative., Then Forgive not Condemn,. Bless not Curse,. Reward not Punish.

Thank you, Dear God, Thank you
B.H., M.A., L.W. Alias "Saint Bill"

Part "E"

Dear Friends. Illusion, The sum total of all Illusion in our mind causes us to waste a lot of time and energy trying to move Mountains, walk on Water, and Raise the Dead. The sum total of all the Illusion in the World, we call the Shadow, or the Devil, or the Satan, or A demon. But they do not exist except as to the Essence of a Shadow (Illusion).

God (Soul) within us is Active and causes us to take Action. But God also gave us a Sense of Judgement to use so that we learn to tell Reality from Illusion, Truth from Lie, Possible from Impossible.

The Sun produces Light and Light allows us to see Reality. From the many Realities of Life, that enter our mind, we begin to have Mutations in the thought process. This we call Creativity.

Now because our mind has no way of knowing what is Possible or what is Impossible of these New Mutations, we have to keep trying to act out the Call (Tempt) of the New mutation: But if you Fail Three (3) times, You say, Three Strikes and you are Out on the Illusion (Shadow) Pile.

With the Mutations you are Successful with, you Add on to the Reality (God) Pile.

You will find that the Reality (God) Pile is the size of Mount Everest, and It Smells like a Rose.

The Illusion (Shadow) Pile is the size of a Mole-Hill, and It stinks like the Waste it is.

So just turn and walk Forward to the Future which is God, which is Reality, which is Life Eternal, which is Good.

Thanks for Listening, Yours Truly,
As ever in, " The Spirit of Goodness"

B.H., M.A., L.W. - ALIAS " SAINT BILL"

PART "F"

Now Friends,. Just before we hear a Song, I want to tell you a little Story,... At Home on the Mantel piece in the Living room there are Four Trophies. Three Gold and One Silver. The first one on the Left side is from " Universal of Canada" where I competed against 100 men across Canada, Selling Educational material, and I came in First place,. Gold Medal.. The second one on the Right side is from the Loyal Protective Life Insurance Co. where I was a Rookie in my first year competing against 200 men across Canada. And I came in Second place,. Silver Medal.. And in the Middle is One from Preview Real Estate Ltd. where I competed against 18 men, and I came in First place,. Gold Medal.

And finally on the Top of all Three is a Gold Medal from Previews Inc., a publishing Co.. I competed against Four Men and One Worm. All Immortals,. Abraham, Buddha, Mohammed, Singh, and of course Robin., And I came in First place,. Gold Medal.

Yes Folks, that was for writing The COM PASS., The Truth,. The EVERLAST TESTAMENT. Now, the other day I was looking at my Mantel piece with my Trophy from Previews Inc. and Institute of Universal Philosophy.

And I put my Foot down Hard on the Worm, and It went to Slitherines and I Rubbed with my Rubber Rubber Heel Until there was nothing left but Dust. And then I said to the other Four,. Bow, you Gentlemen, Bow., Knees and All, You Gentlemen, BOW.

And now my Friends, Family and Children of all ages,. I say, Look Up, and Worship God, the Real, "The Spirit of Goodness",. Not God the Fraud, The Shadow.

And as for Me, You just remember me as the Greatest Salesman and Psychologist that ever walked this Earth.. Yes, My Dear God, The Greatest.

"Saint Bill",... And I want you to know that in God's eye each of you is a "Saint." Isn't that wonderful,. Yes that is wonderful,. Now go and Carry my Torch,... And we will see you all after a while...

Thank you, Yours truly,
As ever in, "The Spirit of Goodness",
B.H., M.A., L.W., Alias, "Saint Bill"

In God's Eye a Day is a Thousand years and a Thousand years is a Day. Therefore, we will see "Our Dear God's Kingdom" Reign the World over by Tomorrow afternoon at this Time. Thank you, Dear God, Thank you.

B.H., M.A., L.W. Alias "Saint Bill".

AN

ETERNAL "TRUST" FOUNDATION

PREVIEWS
Inc.

&

ITS
FOUNDING PARTNERS

Dear Friend,....... Are you the type of Individual first in line to help improve our Nation's psychology? If so, you will be interested in becoming one of our Founding Partners.

We have established an "Eternal (Trust) Foundation". The Object of the (Trust) is: To Relieve Poverty. (Both Physical and Spiritual Poverty). This is an Eternal Need in Humanity, that needs to be Filled by Someone. But since any one person can not do it by his / her own resources, be it Financial, Physical or Spiritual, we are calling on you to contribute your Share toward the Burden.

"Saint Bill", the Founder of the "Trust", has contributed $100,000.00 financially, many Hours of Labor physically, and "The COMPASS" spiritually, as a Track to run on.

We must realize that "A Light in the Night" is a Light in Deed, a "Light in the Light" is a Light in Need. Therefore "A Friend in Need is a Friend in Deed".

Dear Friends,. To be able to Help Others, we must first be able to Help Ourselves. Then as God is Willing there is a Surplus to share with those in Need.

Well, we have herein a Small Apple Tree, 3 foot tall, and next year It will bear Fruit, (Small Apples). This tree will grow to 12 foot tall and bear Large Apples.

But what we Need is an Orchard, and this is where you come in. You can Plant Your tree and It will bear Fruit for you, because you only need Small Apples.

But It will grow Big and there will be a Surplus to Share with Others.

The "Eternal (Trust) Foundation" operating under the name of "Previews Inc." is designed to produce Fruit (REVENUE) and this Revenue will grow and grow, just as the "Trust" will grow and grow.

Now the Net Net Revenue of the " Trust " will be allocated in the following manner.

1) 20% to Charity (To Relieve Poverty) Both Physical and Spiritual Poverty.
2) 25% to Class -B- Voting Shareholders (The descendants of the Founder and the Founding Partners).
3) 40% to Re-Investment so that the "Trust " will grow and grow,. In order to fulfill Its mandate.
4) 15% to the Class-A-Voting Shareholder (Executor) for Administration expenses and services

oooooOooooo

Dear Friend,. In order for the "Eternal (Trust) Foundation" to reach Self-Sufficiency it needs to be valued at $12,215,908.00. Therefore "Saint Bill" the Founder of the Trust is appealing to you to become a "Founding Partner."

Saint Bill" has contributed $100,000.00 to the Trust, and we will call him a One-Star-General.

If you will contribute $500,000.00 to the Trust, we will call you a Five-Star-General. And if you will contribute $2,600,000.00 to the Trust, we will call you a Twenty-Six-Star-General.

This is the maximum we will accept because Charity is Love and to Love is to Give without expecting a Return, and we do not want you to expect a Return other than the Personal Satisfaction of helping your Descendants.

In addition, all Founding Partners will be Eternally Recorded along with "Saint Bill" in the Book of Life, "The Compass".

Please give this your Optimistic consideration and do not hesitate to Say " Let's Do It".

Yours truly,
as ever in, "The Spirit of Goodness"

Previews Inc.
Per: W.J. (Bill) Handel, M.A., L.W. (Coach)

The Charity affiliate:
"Previews Institute of Universal Philosophy"
(Non-Profit)

Note: We have,
Privates at $10,000.00 Corporals at $25,000.00
Sergeants at $50,000.00 and
Lieutenants at $75,000.00

Dear Friends., Let us invest in the Future of Humankind, for a greater degree of Happiness, Decency, Prosperity, and Peace of Mind.

Today's children do not know anything about the Horse and Buggy. Today it is the 797 Jet. Today's children do not know anything about the Sled. Today it is the 4 wheeled Jaguar. Today's children do not know anything about the Sword and Dagger. Today it is "Hands Down" intellect.

So it is with God (The Spirit of Goodness). In the old, old days it was a Vision in the Darkness. Today it is a Vision in the Flood-Lights.

"Saint Bill" has a Vision. A Vision of Happiness, Decency Prosperity, and Peace of Mind throughout the World. "Saint Bill" was brought to the understanding through experience, the best teacher, that if you believe God is Real, you have one. And if you believe that God is an Illusion, you do not have one. And that the same thing applies to the Shadow of God. If you believe that the Shadow is Real, you have one. And if you believe that the Shadow is an Illusion, you do not have one, because It is put out of sight and out of mind, as you have learned to Look Up to God the Real.

Yes, in the not to distant future the unfulfilling influence of the Shadow will be wiped off the face of the Earth, and out of the sight and mind of Humankind.

Yes, the Shadow is a confused Idiot and a Fictional character and a complete Illusion. And does not exist except as to the essence of a Shadow (A nothing, A vacuum of Light)

It says things like "Love your Enemies" out of one side of It's mouth, and Hate Your mother and Father, out of the other side of It's mouth.

It says things like "Have no Doubt and you can walk on Water" or Say to the Mountain "Move" and It will move.

Well, the time has come to wipe these Lies, Illusions and Confusions out of our Minds.

In The COMPASS it says that God says, "Walk around a Lake, and while you are at it enjoy the Scenery. A whole lot of peaceful Truth.

Dear Friends, The COMPASS has 265 pages and we can not retype them all here and now. But you can be assured that Reality is God, and God is Reality, Not Fantasy.

Thanks for Listening; Yours truly,
as ever in, "The Spirit of Goodness"

W.J. (Bill) Handel, M.A., L.W. (Coach)

Alias: "Saint Bill"

FOUNDING PARTNERS

My Summit is My Home & My Home is My Summit
    And My Congregation is My Family

A Home built on "The Spirit of Goodness", "The Spirit of Truth" yes, "The Free Spirit of God" is a Home built for Eternity.

Previews Inc. (Eternal-Trust-Foundation) is a very Small Tree. It has no Branches yet; But next year we hope to see Two branches, and the next year Four more, and the next year Eight more, and so on. The Trunk at the Top will get bigger and bigger. The Roots, above the Clouds, are God's Hands and there are many. Yes, One for each of us.

The Branches are the Legacy of the Founding Partners. The Twigs are our Descendants. And the Apples are the Children that carry the Seed (The Compass). Yes, we will soon have an Orchard.

Founding Partners are those of us who Invest some Riches in the Real Property of the "Eternal-Trust-Foundation" (Previews Inc.); Suggested Min., 25% of the Value of an Up-Down Duplex). Yes, Real Property has Value that never Fades, but rather produces more Value eternally. All to the Glory of God.

Each Founding Partner from now until the year 10,000 B.H. will be Recorded in this Book of Life (The COMPASS). And their Descendants will one day be as Rich as mine will be. And they will give Thanks to God for a Wise Ancestor.

Now then and therefore We will begin the Record.
It will be in Alphabetical order.

No.			Name			Date of Birth

1.

2.

FOUNDING PARTNERS

No.	Name	Date of Birth
1.		
2.		

FOUNDING PARTNERS

No.   Name   Date of Birth

1.

2.

FOUNDING PARTNERS

No.	Name	Date of Birth
1.		
2.		

FOUNDING PARTNERS

No.	Name	Date of Birth

1.

2.

FOUNDING PARTNERS

No.	Name	Date of Birth
1.		
2.		

FOUNDING PARTNERS

No.	Name	Date of Birth
1.		
2.		

FOUNDING PARTNERS

No.	Name	Date of Birth

1. W.J. (Bill) Handel, M.A. LW. March 15/01 B.H.
   Calgary, Canada   One-Star-General

2. T. (Ted) Handel   January 26/-09 B.H.
   Calgary, CAN.   Hon. Twenty-Six-Star-General

3. "Saint Katherina"   Mother of "Saint Bill"
   Tiger Lily, AB.   December 24/-37 B.H.

3. "Saint George"   Father of "Saint Bill"
   Tiger Lily, AB.   July 12/-35 B.H.

FOUNDING PARTNERS

No.	Name	Date of Birth
1.		
2.		

FOUNDING PARTNERS

No.	Name	Date of Birth
1.		
2.		

FOUNDING PARTNERS

No.	Name	Date of Birth
1.		
2.		

FOUNDING PARTNERS

No.   Name   Date of Birth

1.

2.

FOUNDING PARTNERS

No.	Name	Date of Birth

1.

2.

FOUNDING PARTNERS

No.   Name   Date of Birth

1.

2.

FOUNDING PARTNERS

No.	Name	Date of Birth
1.		
2.		

FOUNDING PARTNERS

No.	Name	Date of Birth
1.		
2.		

FOUNDING PARTNERS

No.	Name	Date of Birth

1.

2.

FOUNDING PARTNERS

No.	Name	Date of Birth
1.		
2.		

FOUNDING PARTNERS

No.	Name	Date of Birth
1.		
2.		

FOUNDING PARTNERS

No.	Name	Date of Birth
1.		
2.		

261 T-1

FOUNDING PARTNERS

No.	Name	Date of Birth
1.		
2.		

FOUNDING PARTNERS

No.	Name	Date of Birth
1.		
2.		

FOUNDING PARTNERS

No.	Name	Date of Birth
1.		
2.		

FOUNDING PARTNERS

No.	Name	Date of Birth
1.		
2.		

FOUNDING PARTNERS

No.	Name	Date of Birth
1.		
2.		

FOUNDING PARTNERS

No.	Name	Date of Birth
1.		
2.		

CHAIN of COMMAND

Between
God (the Real) "The Spirit of Goodness",
"Previews Inc."
And
"Previews Institute"

Share Structure of "Previews Inc."
Class-A-Voting (Veto) Shares, Controlling Shares.

Limited to Three,. Held by the "KING" or "QUEEN" of the royal Family of God. Presently known as The President, being: W.J. (Bill) Handel, M.A., L.W.

Class-B-Voting Shares, Equity "Dividend Only" Shares of the Real property of The Royal Family. (Revenue Property)

Presently limited to One Share per Descendant of the Founder and One Share to each Descendant of any and all Founding Partners.

Class-C-Voting Shares, Founding Partner Investment Shares

Unlimited number,. Issued in accordance with the then present Value of the Shares and the size of the investment. At present these are "Mortgage Investment Certificates" secured by Land and Building.

The commitment as to the Dividend or Return on these Shares is met before the Class-B-Share Dividend is calculated.

Class-D-Non-Voting Shares, All the World's population, Friends, Relatives, Acquaintances, And Associates.

These Shares, while Non-Voting in Previews Inc., give you a Vote in the Affairs of Previews Institute, Summit Loc.#002, and the Affairs of any subsequent Summit loc. you belong to from time to time.

These Shares allow you all the Privileges, Benefits, and services that your Summit Local provides from time to time, while you are in Good Standing.

These Shares register you in the "Retirement Income Plan" according to the "Commission Reserve Fund" schedule; Benefit beginning at age 60 yrs.

These Shares are introductory shares and Stepping Stones to a better way in Life. You will find that these Shares are the best thing that have ever come your way, because they introduce you to the Benefit of the Class "C" and Class "B" Shares. They also allow you to make a Charitable Donation to our "Charities Division".

oooooOooooo

Just a little Understanding:

The place of Worship of "Previews Institute" is called a "SUMMIT", the most common of which is our Home. The "Institute" is a charity with Its Objective being to Relieve Poverty. Both Physical and Spiritual poverty.

"Previews Inc." is a private Foundation that will continue to contribute 20% of its Net Net Profit to "Previews Institute" in support of Its Charity work.

"Previews Inc." is the Founding Sponsor of "Previews Institute" and Its members are thereby established as an Eternal Royal Family of God".

Previews Inc. considers each and every last person on Earth a member of The Eternal Royal Family of God; But of course we realize there are ACTIVE and Passive members. But regardless of that, Just for the ASKING any and All of you deserve and will receive the Privileges and Benefits of "PREVIEWISM".

Previews Inc. has four classes of shares: Class-A-Voting, Class-B-Voting, Class-C-Voting, and Class-D-Non-Voting But voting in the affairs of Previews Institute, "Summit Loc. #002" and subsequent Locals.

THe King of The Eternal Royal Family of God, holds all of the Class-A-Voting (3) shares and all of his present descendants each hold One(1) Class-B-Voting share. The Descendants of "Founding Partners" will receive One (1) Class-B-Voting Share. All Founding partners who invest to more quickly let the Foundation grow will hold any number of Class-C-Voting shares according to the size of the investment.

All members of "Previews Institute" will hold a Symbolic Class-D-Non-Voting share in Previews Inc. but receive their Institutional Benefits from the Institute.

Previews Inc. believes in democracy and so there will be votes taken from the shareholders and their wishes Honored in usual circumstance but if the need be the King has a Veto by way of the Class-A-Voting Share.

At "Previews Inc.", the King of The Eternal Royal Family of God, more commonly known as the President or the Executor is responsible for carrying out the Will of the Founder, being W.J. (Bill) Handel, M.A., L.W. Also known as "Saint Bill".

If the Executor or any subsequent Executor is in Breach of Trust then a petition signed by any eleven (11) Class-B-Voting Shareholders will constitute the right to take the Executor to Court and have the Judge decide if He/She is guilty.

If found Guilty, on the first offence there shall be no punishment but He/She will be warned that if He/She is found Guilty a second time He/She will be Impeached. Meaning He/She will be removed from Office.

In the event that a King or Queen (Executor) is removed from Office in this procedure, then the Oldest descendant of The Founder shall be sworn in as Executor, President, King of The Eternal Royal Family of God,. Provided however that He/She is not over Sixty (60) years of age and provided firstly that He/She is a Devoted PREVIEWLITE. This means that the Oldest Previewlite Descendant Sixty (60) yrs. or under is eligible to take the Office of Executor of the Eternal Estate (Foundation) called "Previews Inc." whose Will it is to Grow and Grow to keep up with the Family and to continue to Contribute Twenty (20%) per cent of Its Net Net Profits to "Previews" Institute" so that "Previews Institute" will also be Eternal and never cease to function, as a Charity and a "Summit" with Its object being "To Relieve Poverty". (Both physical and Spiritual poverty).

P.S., A Devoted and committed PREVIEWLITE is a person who worships "The Spirit of Goodness" (God) as manifested in and by "The COMPASS".

In the event that a "Devoted Previewlite Descendant" does not step forward for the Position, Then The Chairman of the Board of "Summit Loc. #001" shall appoint a Devoted Previewlite as "Executor" of the Estate, "Previews Inc.", and He/She will hold Office until such time that a "Devoted Previewlite Descendant" steps forward to assume the responsibilities of Executor, President, and King of "The Eternal Royal Family of God" as manifested in and by The COMPASS.

If All else fails then The Judge shall appoint an Unbiased, Non-Partisan person to assume the responsibilities of "Executor" to fulfill the Will of The Founder. This person shall hold Office until a "Devoted Previewlite Descendant" of the Founder steps forward to assume the Office of the Executor, President, and King of The Eternal Royal Family of God, as manifested in and by "The COMPASS.

P.S., With the exception of Embezzlement, all breaches of trust will be punishable on the second offence according to the above and according to the Law.

Embezzlement shall be punishable on the first offence according to the above, and according to the Law.

Previews Institute of Universal Philosophy

The Official Representative of "Previews Institute" Summit Loc. #001 (H.O.) shall be Its "Chairman of the Board" otherwise known as Its "Chief Executive" or "Executive Director".

Both "Previews Inc." and "Previews Institute" understand and agree that "Previews Institute" Summit Loc. #001 (H.O), shall have a maximum of Eleven (11) members (them being the Board of Directors) and that the King or Queen of "Previews Inc." is a permanent sitting member on the "Board of Directors" of "Previews Institute".

Both "Previews Inc." and "Previews Institute" understand and agree that "Previews Inc." shall have One (1) Director, that being the King or the Queen of "Previews Inc.", and One(1) Advisor, that being the "Chief Executive" of "Previews Institute" Summit Loc. #001 (H.O.).

The Director (Executor) of "Previews Inc.", that being the King or Queen of "Previews Inc." will have further advice and directives from Its "Class-B-Voting" Shareholders, over which "The Executor" has a Veto power by way of His/Her "Class-A-Voting Shares".

All Subsequent "Summit Loc's #002, #003, #004, etc. etc. of "Previews Institute" will be subservient to "Summit Loc. #001 (H.O.) of "Previews Institute".

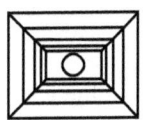

PREVIEWISM
Our World is Beautiful, Yes, Multi-Cultural

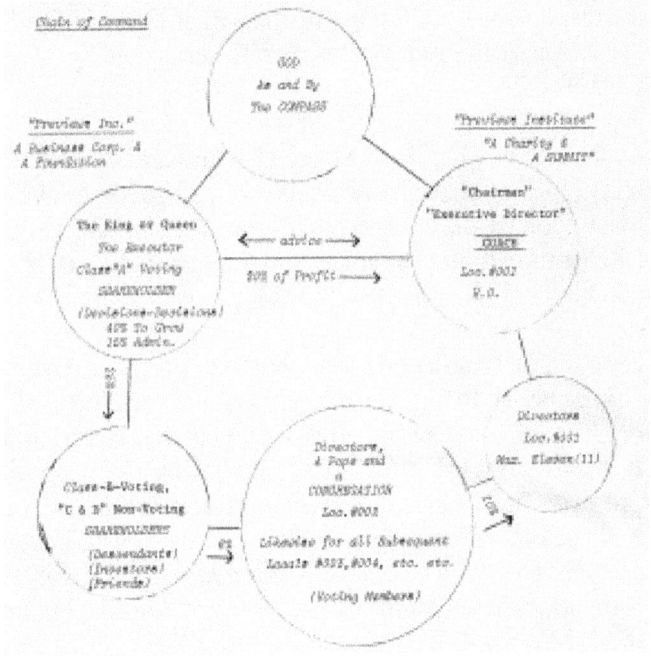

THE TRADITION OF "CHANGE FOR THE BETTER" IS BORN IN
"PREVIEWISM"

---

www.previews-inc.com
Make 10 - 20 Copies per week and Pass It On. - God will be well Pleased.

ooooo**O**ooooo

The Messiah of the "Previewlite" (Previewism) is the King or Queen, in "Waiting", of Previews Inc.. Not the King or Queen (Executor) of Previews Inc., but the King or Queen, in "Waiting", a Living Being, being prepared for the responsibility of Executing the will of God (the Real) "The Spirit of Goodness" as manifested in and by "The COMPASS".

Yes, the Newly Defined "Messiah" is now a Living Being and not a Fictional Character. Is that not Wonderful, yes, that is wonderful, We now have the Real and Living Hope and Promise of improvement and progress for All of Humankind.

Is that not wonderful, yes, that is wonderful Every Humanbeing, In the World, approximately age forty (40) or older and not over sixty (60) is eligibly to prepare Him/Her self for the position of Executor (King or Queen) of Previews Inc.. and He/She will hold office until His/Her body ceases to function. He/She will then go to Heaven as a "SAINT with a purpose." Naturally there are other Limitations in the beginning but in the not to distant Future this is how it will Be.

Thank you, Yours truly,
As ever in, "The Spirit of Goodness"
B.H., M.A., L.W., (Saint Bill)

ooooo**O**oooo

"THE OVERLAP to THE SERMONS"
November 16/59 B.H.

Dear Friends,. Thank you, Thank you,. You may be Seated. To begin today, We have a Question for you,. Why does god provide us with Prophecies, (Previews of the Future),?.......
Answer: so that we can work toward Fulfilling them. Yes, god has a Plan and the Previews that It gives us are a part of the Plan that we are to Fulfil. We all have Previews everyday and today We want to share a Preview with you.

In the not to distant Future you are going to realize that you are a "Saint" in god's eye. Yes, you are a Saint, because God created you with a "Good Nature" in god's Image. And everyday God forgives you and washes away the Bad and leaves you "Spotless" in God's Eye. Yes you are a Saint in God's Eye, and God Loves you, and gives you Its Blessings.

The Accuser (The Shadow) says you are a "Sinner", You are Bad,. You must Pay, and live in Misery...If you do not have any Money, you must Bow Down and worship me "Totally" or you go to Hell.

But you must Remember, The Accuser is a Liar and has no Power and can not send you to Hell or to Heaven.

God prepared a Spot for you in Heaven upon your conception,. And because God Loves you, God is prepared to Forgive you all your Errors and Sins against Humanity, and keep you "Spotless". Yes, you are a Saint in God's Eye.

The Accuser (The Shadow) says your Errors are Sins against God., But you must remember the Accuser is a Liar; God is never Offended by any One or any thing. god always Understands and Forgives and keeps you spotless,. So that you will be Fit to take your place in Heaven... Oh, Yes, That is Right, there is Nothing or No-one that can stop you from going to Heaven, because God always gets the Last Word.,

And the Last Word is... "Forgiven"...... And the Shadow (Accuser) can go to Hell by Itself.

Yes, God always gives us Prophecies (Previews of the Future), But there is a Problem. God's Servants are Human and so they sometimes make Good (True) prophecies and sometimes they make Bad (False) prophecies.

But there is a Solution: We have to use our "Sense of Judgement" and decide which is a Good prophecy and which is a Bad prophecy. (True or False)... And then we work toward fulfilling the Good prophecies, Not the Bad.

If we work toward fulfilling the Bad prophecy, We are working for the Shadow, Not God.
Example,. If a Prophet says that God wants Someone to be Killed to satisfy God's thirst for Vengeance,. It is obvious that it is a False prophecy, because God
does not want us to Kill. Yes, God does not want a Sacrifice,. God wants Obedience to Its Good prophecies. (And says, Forgiven, if you fail to Obey)

Example,. If a Prophet says, that God wants us to find or prepare an Earthly Ruler that is capable of bringing Heaven to Earth,. That would be a good (True) prophecy, and one worthy of our Effort to work toward achieving Heavenly conditions on Earth for the Ruler to maintain.

Another Example of a Bad prophecy: If a Prophet says, that god wants us to find or prepare a Heavenly Ruler from Earth to go to Heaven and Rule in Heaven,. That would be a Bad (False) prophecy, because, Firstly, We do not know anything about conditions in Heaven and Secondly, God is quite capable of Ruling in Heaven on Its own.. God does not need an Uninformed Human to mess things up in Heaven.

So you see, we should not try to be God, we should only try to be Godly (Good) Humans, and work toward bringing heaven to Earth.

Yes, Folks, a Prophet of God, prophecize and says, there will soon be Happiness, Decency, prosperity, and Peace of Mind throughout the World.

A Prophert of the Shadow, prophecize and says, there will soon be Sodomy, Drunkenness, Perversion, and Abomination throughout the World.

God gave you a "Sense of Judgement" so that you can decide correctly which prophecy you want to and should Fulfill. It is obvious, Is it not.

Yes, God says,. You are a "Saint", now go and act Accordingly.

The Shadow says,. You are a "Sinner", now go and act Accordingly.

Which do you want to Believe?.... Well, Folks, we choose to believe God, and we are Happy-Go-Lucky with It.

Now God says, "A Mountain is a Mountain" and "A Molehill is a Molehill".

The Shadow makes, "A Molehill out of a Mountain" and "A Mountain out of a Molehill".

Yes, There are so many False prophets....
There is Only one "TRUE" prophet, and that is "The Spirit of Goodness" with all of Its children. The oldest of which is" The Spirit of Truth", and th e Youngest of which is "The Spirit of Enthusiasm."

And We have it says, "Saint Bill", and the Spirit of Preserverance is related to the Spirit of Enthusiasm and we have them Both, says "Saint Bill". And the Spirit of Love is related to Perserverance and we have them all Three, says "Saint Bill". And the Spirit of Truth is related to Love and we have them all Four, says "Saint Bill".

Yes, we must develop the Characteristics of "The Spirit of Goodness" to make us Strong.

Now we are not saying that we are the Strongest among Us. But we are saying we are the Happiest among Us,. And we would rather be Happy, than Strong.

We let God be Strong, So that we will be Happy.

Note: If you take an Orange, you have the Good inside and the Peel is the Waste. If you take a Banana, you have the Good inside and the Peel is the Waste. So it is with Humankind. The Good we do from within stands Forever.. The Bad we do on the Outside, God considers Waste,. Not Bad, Just Waste. But god does not let Waste go to Waste. The Waste is turned into Fertilizer over time and is Good.

So you see, there is no Bad in God's world, Only Good.

All except for One thing. yes, the Shadow. The Shadow is total Waste of Time with Its Lies and Illusions, and Counterfeit Miracles,. Designed to disintegrate your Sense of Judgement, so that you do not know Right from Wrong, Good from Waste, or True from False.

Yes, "look Up" and see and hear God speaking, and then Obey God., (The True Prophet).

Thanks again for Listening,

Yours truly, as ever in, The Spirit of Goodness,.

"Saint Bill".

DESCRIPTION
of
HEAVEN
(Visual & Written)

The Centre circle is the top of God's Umbrella. It is called the "SUN" (A Steel-Glass-Ball). It showers us with "Light", (knowledge (Truth).
The Second circle is the Earth's Orbit around the "SUN".
The Big (Outside) circle is the Sky around the Earth, and the Flat Surfaces are the Six corners (Sides) of the Earth, And the little 1/6th circles are the Sky (God's Umbrella) over us. (Yes, You are never Outside God's Umbrella.)
The Big (Outside) circle is also the Outermost Perimeter of the Universe, EnCompassing Heaven, where we Sit with our Back to Outer-Darkness and our Face to Inner-Light, Where we See the Planets, the Stars, the Moons, and of course the "SUN" in the Centre,. Which also allows us to See every Little Speck of Dust and All else that is moving on the Face of the Earth.

And so we Sit and Gigle, Chat, and Watch the World go by. (Glory, Glory,. Halleluiah!!)

Yes, Just Beautifull,. How about that, Eh!!

oooooOooooo

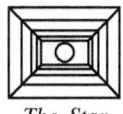

PREVIEWISM
Our World is Beautiful, Yes, Multi-Cultural

The Star of PREVIEWS

Author: "SAINT BILL"
Revealed By: "The Spirit of Truth"

Because The Amphitheatre of God (Heaven) has a Tier for Every Language
God Speaks with Actions from Centre Stage.

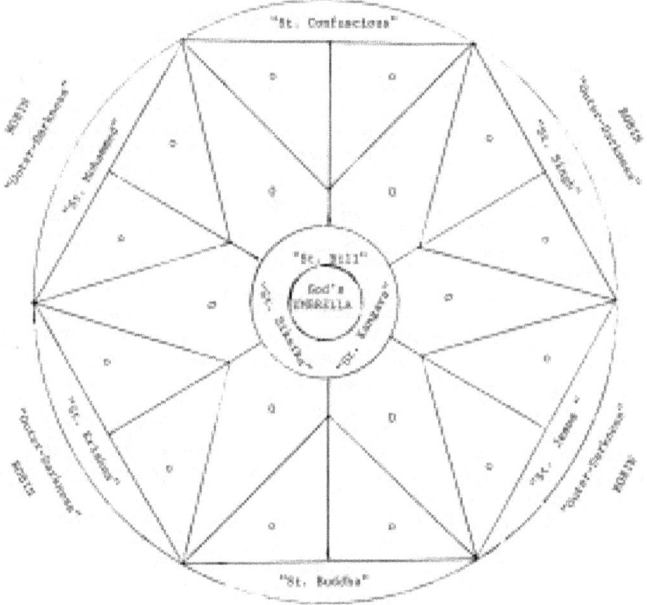

God's UMBRELLA Extends over ALL of US,
According TO "The COMPASS" (The EverLast Testament)

The STAR of Multiculturalism

"Specializing in "Food for THOUGHT"   Since (51 A.B.)
4209 - 26th Avenue S.E., Calgary, Alberta T2B OE1
*THE TRADITION OF "CHANGE FOR THE BETTER" IS BORN IN
PREVIEWISM*

THE STEM
of
GOD'S UMBRELLA

See Chapter 3, of The COMPASS, Part "C" Vs. 16-17, Page 46-part 47.

Yes, It is a Big Picture when you see It from Heaven. Yes, from the Outside In, which is from the Bottom Up, and not from the Top of the Earth Down.

Yes, "Look Up" and see the Big Picture.

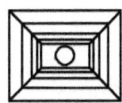 *PREVIEWISM*
Our World is Beautiful, Yes, Multi-Cultural

PREVIEWS of the FUTURE

God's UMBRELLA Extends over ALL of US,
According to "The COMPASS" (The Everlast Testament

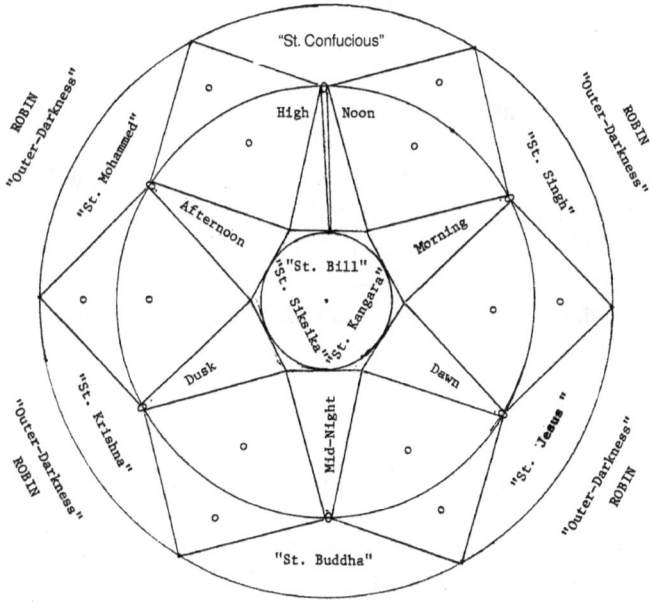

Because The Amphitheatre of God (Heaven) has a Tier for
Every Language
God Speaks with Actions from Centre Stage.

The STAR of Multiculturalism
"INSIDE-OUT"

"Specializing in "Food for THOUGHT"   Since (51 A.B.)

My Children and My Friends the World over.

In the Beginning there was "The Spirit of Goodness" (God the Real), and it was Dark and Cold., And god said, "Let there be Angels", and from One there became a Multitude of Angels around God., And God said, I shall call you My Children,. yes, My Little "Spirits" of Goodness.

All of the Angels obeyed and Honored god, "Except One"., And this One said, "I am God", Obey and Honor Me and I will take you to Heaven.

Then the Little Children said, "Where are we Now",. And after a moment god said, I will "Show" you,... Let there be Light,. And the Light appeared in the Midst of them,. And the Angels seen they were in Heaven around the Universe of Planets, Stars, Moons, and Space, and they Knew "The One" had tried to Deceive them.

Then the Angels said, Let us All Join Hands in One Big Circle around "Our Magnificent god" and Praise God for our Creation in Its Image., And "The One" Disobedient disappeared into Outer-Darkness behind them for Fear of being Exposed.

And the Angels said, We shall call "That One", The Shadow, in reference to the Darkness Behind us., And we shall call God, "Light", in recognition of the Knowledge Before us.. And the Source of God we shall call, " The Eclipse of Energy", around the "Steel-Glass-Ball" (the Sun) in the Centre.

Then god said, I shall give you, All my children, a Name so that you remember that you are All Related to me (God the Real),. And each of you shall have a Shadow below and Behind you. My first Born I shall call "Truth" The Youngest I shall call "Enthusiasm".

Note: This the first Piece of the Picture We have of the Beginning.

...And the Last shall come First, and the First shall come Last. And God is, was, and always shall be the Same, Today, and Tomorrow,. and with No missing link,. what is thought of the missing link is Illusion,. Small and Invisible and Insignificant. Yes, Cast it out, because We are One with God, and God is One with Us, Always.

And So you see, when your Body ceases to function, You go to Meet your Soul-Mate in Heaven with God.

Thank you, Yours truly,
As ever in, "The Spirit of Goodness",
B.H., M.A., L.W., (Saint Bill)

THE END
oooooOoooo
"YES"
So It is Written
So Shall It BE
oooooOooooo

THE
PREVIEWLITE
CATECHISM

THE PREVIEW LITE CATECHISM

1. **Introduction**
   Dear is My God's Name
   Yes, My God's Name is Dear to me.

2. **First Commandment**
   "Keep your Eye and Attention on Reality",
   because Reality is God and God is Reality,
   Not Fantasy.

3. **Declaration:**
   Yes, I believe in a God of Truth and Reality,
       a God of Goodness
       a God of Love and Forgiveness
       a God of Future
       a God of Enthusiasm
       a God of Pride in Accomplishment
       a God of Increasing and Improving
       Yes, a God Alive
       Yes, God is the "Spirit of Goodness"
       And has many Good Characteristics.
       Ch 10, vs 1, Ch 11, vs 10-19
       Thank you Dear God Thank you.

4. **Confessional Creed:**
   I do not believe in Counterfeit Miracles.
   Counterfeit Miracles are supposed
   happenings that break the Laws of God (or
   nature) and therefore are outside the Laws of
   God and Lies of the Shadow. God's works are
   all within the Laws of God and as such are
   Real. A miracle in

God's Eye is just an unusual or rare happening, but within the Laws of God and therefore True.

5.   Footnotes:

a.   Applied Faith, based on Experience, has a sense of Judgement and Reason, and is very susceptible to the Voice of God, because God is Truth. Blind Faith, based on Supposition, has no sense of Judgement or Reason, and is very susceptible to the Voice of the Shadow, because Shadow is Lie, and Lie or Shadow relies on One's lack of Judgement or Reason, to flourish.

b.   What does the word "Believe" mean? To Believe means, to Be or to Do or to Live Out. So if you say, I believe I can build a House...You build a house and you prove you believe you can build a house. But if you say, I believe I can walk on water...You are lying to yourself and you know it is a Lie before you try to prove it. And the Shadow wants you to lie to yourself because it is the Ultimate of disgrace. Yes, to lie to someone else is one thing but to lie to Oneself, that is the ultimate of Confusion. And that is what the Shadow wants, Confusion,...Illusion and Confusion.

c.   If you say you believe something and do not Try to Do it, then you become a person of many words and no actions. Or All Preach and No Practice, or Hypocrite, Fraud, Illusion, Liar.

d. Also if you are in doubt as to whether something is true or not, Try it and you will find the Truth is a possibility and you will succeed. But a Lie is an impossibility and you will fail.

e. When you find an impossibility do not Lie and say it is possible. No, accept it as a guideline or law of God that is not to be broken. Remember that No-one can break the Guidelines or Laws or Impossibilities of God, except the Shadow; and the reason the Shadow can break the Laws or Impossibilities of God is because It Lies. It, the Shadow, cooks up a Counterfeit Miracle and says it is a Success-Story. And then says Believe Me, I am God, I am God, Please I love you.

f. So there you are, You have your choice. You can believe the Shadow and live a lie and be totally frustrated and confused all your life, or You can remember that God can not and will not break Its own Laws. That is right, God does not have a double standard. God lives by Its Laws just as you must and God gives you many and sufficient Possibilities to have fun with and Learn to be successful with, within the Guidelines and or Laws of God.

g. And One thing more, God knows that the Wise person has a very keen sense of Judgement and sense of Reason based upon experience and truth upon truth upon truth. But if a wise person believes a Lie, knowing it is a Lie, he/she is disrupting, disintegrating and destroying his/her sense of Judgement and Reason and falling into Confusion. This is why the insidious Shadow says, Please Believe this One Lie, it is Harmless; then very soon another and another, Yes, Lie upon Lie upon Lie, and Illusion upon Illusion upon Illusion.

h. God says, Preach Truth and only Truth and remember God's laws can not be broken in Truth but Only in Lie. And also remember, God only produced Two Miracles and they are, Firstly, God formulated the Universe and all that is in it, on it and around it. Secondly, God manifested Itself in the Human mind. That is it, that is all, anything further to this is Counterfeit (of the Shadow).

6. REGARDING UNCONDITIONAL LOVE & FORGIVENESS:
We must remember, God Loved, Loves, and will always love us First. We do not love God First. We love God after It loves us. In the beginning God loves us and sets us Free to "Reap what we Sow". God does not stop loving us when we do wrong. (ch 5, vs 7) No, God is unconditionally forgiving and unconditionally loving. That is why it is said, that the Sun shines on the Good and the Bad; And the Rain falls on the Good and the Bad. But God gave us a Sense of Judgement and a Sense of Reason to exercise daily so that we can learn to avoid the pitfall of watching the Shadow and subsequently walk the Path of Righteousness of and with God; And not have to suffer needlessly.

7. **The Infinite Expanse of God:**

Wanting and Gaining Wisdom is of God Being satisfied with Ignorance is of the Shadow.

1. Shadow says, Listen to No-One, except Me, I am God, I am God.
God says, Listen to Everyone, and take the Wheat, that being the Good, and leave the Chaff, that being the Waste.

God is not limited to any one person's knowledge of it. But rather, God is so diverse that it reveals Itself as Unique to each of us on earth. And so the Compass is a general overall Underview of God, but if we took the interpretations of every Human being in the World and put them all together we would have an Underall Overview of God on High to the extent of Its present stage of Its manifestation in the Humansphere.

Although God has an Arm stretched out to each of us on earth there are a few common denominators we all share. To mention just a few, They are: God is Truth, Shadow is Lie. God is Reality, Shadow is Illusion. God is Good Actions, Shadow is Bad Actions. God is Love and Compassion, Shadow is Fear and Hate.
God Leads us to Blessings,
Shadow leads us to Punishment.

8. **The Foremost Characteristics of God are:**
Ch. 1, pg. 4, vs. 16.
1. God is Good (Has a Good Nature)
2. God is Unconditionally Loving.
3. God is Unconditionally Forgiving.
4. God is Intangible.
5. God is not totally Comprehendable.
6. God is a Positive, Formulative, and Productive Force.
7. God is not Vengeful.
8. God is not Jealous.
9. God does not Fear Anything, Therefore God is Not to be Feared, but Loved.
10. God does not Judge against us. (Never)
11. God is Unique. Yet is Unique to Each of Us.
12. God can only be tempted to do Good and God will only Tempt us to do Good.
13. God can Not be Defined, Described by/ or Related to/or as anything Physical. Not in any Sense. Not one Speck of Physical Form (Characteristic) God is a Spiritual or Mental Image (Form) in Every Sense of any Good Word.

9. **We have hereinbefore described the** Characteristics of God that allow us to achieve most readily, the Intangible benefits and Joys of Life. Now we will look at the Characteristics of God that most readily allow us to achieve, in abundance, the Tangible things in Life.
Ch. 1, pg. 11, vs. 26. Ch. 11, pg. 83, vs. 10-19

1.	Sincerity	2.	Knowledge
3.	Planning	4.	Enthusiasm
5.	Organization	6.	Determination
7.	Confidence	8.	Industry
9.	Perseverance	10.	Moderation
11.	Happiness	12.	Silence
13.	Appreciation	14.	Chastity
15.	Fair Play	16.	Tolerance
17.	Charity	18.	Pride & Humility
19.	Be Lucky	20.	Judgement
21.	Feeling as Unique in God as God is Unique in You.		

With respect to your "Traits of Character" that you want to acquire or improve upon. You list them and then take one at a time, describe it on a Pocket Card, and carry it with you to read while you Practice it for One week. Then take the next Trait, describe it and Practice it for one Week. Continue the process until you cover them all and repeat until you are strong in them all.

10. **The Basic Truths and Values** that have been with us since time began, when God first manifested Itself in Humankind, and which are complimentary to our God and Its nature. They are that a person should: Ch. 1, pg. 9, vs. 24.

   1) Acknowledge, Respect and Remember, his/her True God of, Good, Love, and Forgiveness, in his/her Prayers of Thanks to God for his/her

Health and well being. (Spiritually, Physically, and Mentally) and for the Good things in life that come our way. (Tangible or Intangible).

2) Not use Profane language with or about people or your God.

3) Take a couple of days off per week. (Things Do improve don't they, it will not be long before we take three (3) days off)

4) Honor your Father and Mother, and Elders. 5) Not kill anyone, Especially not yourself.

6) Honor your Word and make your Word your Bond.

7) Reap from the Produce of your own Seeding.

8) Not spread derogative or untrue information about a person.

9) Love Humankind as God loves you.

10) In the Initiative, Treat others as you would like to be treated, and in the response, Treat others as they treat you, and even more so. That is to say, "If someone treats you Good, you treat them Better" and "If someone treats you Bad, you treat them Worse".

11) Practice the Good, the positive, the constructive and the productive (etc.) things in life, both in the Innerself and Outerself and in the Tangible and Intangible things of the world.

12) Not be tempted into anything that is Bad according to the forgoing or your understanding of what brings Bad. (In other words use Moderation, and your sense of judgement and sense of balance).

13) Gather often to Celebrate and Praise The True God of Good, Love and Forgiveness.
(When you Celebrate or praise, do it in a Circle(s) (Standing, Sitting, etc., does not matter) but in a circle to signify the benevolent Image of God. And to Signify that life is, or can be a benevolent Circle, as opposed to a vicious circus. You know what I mean. Do this from the heart and with enthusiasm and it will cost you nothing. Because what you "sow" you "Reap" manifold.
14) First and foremost, teach your children about these Facts of Life and God, according to the Truth, the Whole Truth, and nothing but the Truth, and God will help you........,   So,......Between the Lines.

11. God "Never" Judges against you; God always says, "Not Guilty".: See, Ch. 8, pg. 65, vs. 21-26. Ch. 5, pg. 52, vs. 7. Ch. 9, pg. 73, vs. 12.

12. Love God Above All Things, and remember God is not Perfect; God is Alive, Active and Good, Ever-increasing, Ever-improving, Excellent, Very Flexible and Easily Pleased. Ch. 2, pg. 37, vs. 52.

13. We, Humanbeings, are Born with a Good Nature (God's Nature) Inherently.
Ch. 1, vs. 4-6. Ch. 1, vs. 14-15.

14. We, Humanbeings, communicate directly with God. God is quite capable of handling Its own affairs. It does not need a Middleman, that being

a Shadow.
Ch. 1, vs. 18.

15. To gain "Trust" in God, Look Up to and Above the Horizon.
Ch. 1, vs. 40. Ch. 3, pg. 42 - 46

16. Since we are by Nature Good and we receive Unconditional love from God and Its Unconditional Forgiveness, Humankind need only learn not to develop Guilt Complexes and the subsequent Fear of God, by refusing to have   any Guilt trips put over It by anyone, anything, or especially oneself; but
rather......con't..........
Ch. 1, pg. 6, vs. 19

17. God is Future, The Future, Our Future, And The Future Looks Bright Ahead:

God says, All my children, Yellow, Red, Black, White and Brown, throughout the world will meet me in Heaven. (the Rich, the Poor, the Good and the Seemingly Bad.)
Ch. 2, pg. 37, vs. 54.

God says, there are no discriminations, nor prerequisites for entering Heaven.
Ch. 2, pg. 38, vs. 55
God says, the rules and regulations I have given you to follow, are not   meant as prerequisites to heaven but rather given that you can enjoy a little

bit of heaven while you are here on earth.
Ch. 2, pg. 38. vs. 56.

And when you are finished with your physical life here on earth, Your Spirit (Soul) enters your Spiritual Life with God in Heaven and like God you are Blessed with Eternal Life with God.

God says, When your physical body dies, your Spirit does not die but rather comes to Heaven immediately, to take Its place in that Outer most Big Big Circle around Our Magnificent God.(Ch. 2, pg. 38, vs. 57. • Ch. 9, pg. 77, vs. 17.)

Poste Script

The Shadow says, You are all Condemned to Death.
God says, Hog Wash, You are all Blessed with Life upon Life upon Life. There is no Death in God's world, Just Life after Life after Life. To Hell with the Shadow's negative, faithless, hopeless mindset (attitude).

Thank you Dear God Thank you
B.H., M.A., L.W. "Saint BILL".

For Harmony
In every Facet of Human Relations
Remember: Your God is as Valid as Mine.
But: The Shadow is Illusion.

The Prayer of "Saint Bill"
(All together now, too.)

My Dear God in Heaven, In the World,
And in my Heart, Mind and Soul,
I Love you, I Love you, and I,
Thank you for "The Compass," for
Thy Kingdom has come by it and
Thy Will, is now done on Earth as it is in Heaven.
Let us remember to "Look Up" in our daily activities
Let us forgive one another as thou hast forgiven us
Thank you for letting me remember to everyday more
and more please you, for it is to my advantage
Thank you for my daily Bread
Thank you for my Health and Well Being
In Spirit, Body and Mind
Thank you for All my Blessings (recount)
Thank you for my Family and Friends (recount)
Thank you for making me Happy go Lucky
Thank you for Reserving a Spot for me in Heaven,
Dear God,
Thank you for All things Good
For Thine is the Kingdom, the Power and the Glory,
For ever and Ever.
Amen, Amen and Amen.

P.S.: Routine Grace before a Meal.
Thank you, Dear God, for coming to be Our Guest,
and Letting this Food to us be Blessed. Amen.

The Purpose of God, and thereby
The Objects of the "PREVIEWLITE"

1) To make and keep people Happy go Lucky.
2) To keep people Free of Guilt, Fear, Doubt and Illusion.
3) To set in people a frame of Mind to achieve the above.
4) To bring people to live in Harmony with one another.
5) To bring people to leave this world a better place than when they came into it.
6) To distribute the wealth and abundance of Gods' Food and Essentials of life to the Needy throughout the world.
7) To bring "The Gospel of Saint BILL", that being "The Free Spirit of God", "The Spirit of Truth", Yes, "The Spirit of Goodness" as manifested in and by "The Compass" to the World at large and to organize, co-ordinate and direct the Energies of Its' 5.1 Billion members in the same direction at the same time, for a Loving Force to be Reckoned with, to the Glory of God.
8) To bring "Heaven to Earth" so that we might enjoy a little of Heaven while we are here on Earth.

9) To foster and develop among Its' members and the World at large a recognition of the importance of the "Good Natured God" in their life and for they themselves to foster and develop their "Good Nature" as a compliment to Our Dear God.

10) To organize and provide religious instruction, and to perform pastoral work.

11) To establish and maintain buildings for worship and other religious use.

12) To Place a copy of "The COMPASS" in every Home in every Country of the World, as soon as possible, by Sale and/or by Gift.

13) In Summary: To Relieve poverty.
(Both Physical and Spiritual poverty.)

Dear Friends in "Saint BILL",............ We are CELEBRATING a NEW BEGINNING, ...Based on the Facts, Yes, Truth and Reality,. Not Supposition or Illusions and Lies. Because God speaks with Actions,. Not with Words,. Yes, Actions speak Louder than words.

THE TRUE COVENANT OF GOD

Out of an Age of light,. Not an Age of Darkness

a) God has Promised us that It will not Condemn or Curse anyone, Ever.

b) God has Promised us Forgiveness, Unconditionally, because It has a "Good nature", and to preserve Our " Good Nature".

c) God has Promised us that because It is Ever understanding, It will never be Offended or Alienated by anyone,. So as not to give any cause for Guilt or Fear.

d) God has Promised us ALL a Spot in Heaven regardless of how we Worship,. because God Set us Free,. But as such the Law is, What you Sow, You Reap, manifold on Earth.

e) God has Promised to Love each and everyone of us Equally,. So as not to give any cause for Jealousy or Hate.

f) God has Promised us ALL a "Sense of Judgement" to use,. So as to help one another to grow in Reality and Truth.

g) God has Promised us All many more such Good and Wonderful characteristics,. So as to allow us to Live and Enjoy life to the fullest.

"Our Dear God" as manifested in and by The COMPASS receives our Thanks for these and many more such Promises.

Prepared by: "Saint BILL"

Verification

Gen. 1, v.16 - (LIE)
Gen. 22, v. 1 - (LIE)
Ex. 34, v. 14 - (LIE)
Judg. 9, v.23 - (LIE)
Nahu. 1, v. 2n - (LIE)
Math. 17, v. 20 - (LIE)
Math. 14, v. 29 - 31 - (LIE)
Lk. 14, v. 26 - (LIE)
Jn. 14, v. 12 - (½ TRUTH)
Eph. 5, v. 29 - (½ TRUTH)
1 Cor. 13, v. 4 & 7 - (TRUTH)
2 Th. 2, v. 9 - (TRUTH)
2 Th.2, v.11 - (LIE)
Jam. 1, v. 4 - (LIE)
1 Jn. 4, v. 8 & 16-20 (TRUTH)
Eph. 4, v. 26 - (TRUTH)
Math 5, v. 48 - (LIE)
Rev. 22, V.3 - (TRUTH)
Acts 26, v. 16-18 - (TRUTH)
1 Cor. 13, v. 8-13 (TRUTH)
JN. 7, v. 16-18 (TRUTH)

The following is a Chronological list of the "King" or "Queen" of "The Eternal Royal Family of God" as manifested in and by The COMPASS. That being the Head of "Previews" beginning with the Founder. The Base year being 5939 A.M.

The Successors hereof shall be added in Perpetuity, and the First shall come Last, and the Last shall come First.

1)   Saint BILL, W.J. (Bill) Handel, M.A. L.W.
       Born: 01 B.H.   R: 54 B.H. to 75 B.H.

2)   Saint GREG,   Gregory Handel
       Born: 33 B.H.   R: 75 B.H. to

oooooOooooo

<u>God has Three (3) main Powers</u>.
1) Power of Creation.
2) Power of Evolution.
3) Power of Suggestion.

oooooOooooo

<u>How strong are you in your particular Faith in God?</u>

1) Strong.   Then you can read The COMPASS and it will not bother you a Bit.
2) Weak.   Then you can read The COMPASS and it will strengthen you.

oooooOooooo

<u>The Difference between a "Shadow Worshipper" and a "Previewlite"</u>

The Shadow worshipper is walking on a Tight Rope across the "Grand Canyon". (He/She is playing with Insanity.)

The Previewlite is walking on a Bridge, 26 feet wide, with 4 foot Side-rails to guide you. The Side-rails are your Sense of Judgement and Sense of Reason. (You should never go anywhere without them).

Now when the wind comes The Previewlite bends and weaves and sways but continues on his/her way across the way.

Now when the wind comes The Shadow Worshipper finds there are no Side-rails, (No Sense of Judgement or Sense of Reason) and so he/she falls on his/her pointed Head.

Yes, the one is Living in Reality (a firm foundation) The other is Living in a "Little Glass House" also known as a "little Bubble" (a big ILLUSION) and when the wind comes it bursts.

(Ha, Ha, HA, HA, HA, HA, HA, HA, HA, HA, HA, HA, Chuckle, Chuckle, I had to Laugh.)

oooooOooooo

God is young and Very Wise and never Contradicts Itself because It Understands the whole Picture.

The Shadow is a Confused Idiot and Contradicts Itself on every turn. Yes, from one side of Its mouth It says, "Love your enemies", and from the other side of Its mouth It says, "Hate your Mother and Father". Yes, complete Confusion.

oooooOooooo

Question:	Why did God create Humankind?
Answer-1)	So that It would have a warm place to stay, a place to call Home, on Earth. (While on Vacation.)
Answer-2)	So that It could have many Grandchildren, because It liked lots of Company in Heaven.

oooooOooooo

B.H., M.A., L.W., "Saint Bill"

oooooOooooo

THINGS TO REMEMBER

1. God Never Retaliates.
   (NO Consequences from God)

2. Humankind Retaliates, because It sometimes listens to the Shadow (Illusion): Which says, God punishes. (Lie)

3. When they listen to God, they Forgive. Because God always says, Forgiven, or Not Guilty.

4. God does not Fear because Fear has to do with Punishment and Punishment has to do with Hate. And God does not Hate. God Loves and Forgives. And hands out Blessings.
   (No Consequences from God)

oooooOooooo

oooooOooooo

Question: What is the Difference between God and the Humanbeing?

Answer: God is both Young and old, both Innocent and Wise and Far Far ahead of us, and always Understands our mistake because It has already been there, and so always Loves and forgives, which is Good. All because It has not, does not and will not Look at, or Acknowledge the Shadow.

The Humanbeing in the Following have to Learn to Cope with, Deal with and Overcome the Unfulfilling influence of the Shadow (Illusion). Because It causes frustration and pain. But once done, the Humanbeing is much like God except that It is Far Far Behind, Yes, Always in the Following. But when the Body ceases to function, we meet God, take the Last step and become Just Like God.

oooooOooooo

oooooOooooo

A BLESSING over your Head sets you Free and Freedom gives you Courage to fulfil your Ambitions (Dreams). Because of the promise of goodness.

So you are Servant and Master in One of your God.

A CURSE over your Head instills Fear and Fear inhibits your Ambitions (Dreams) because of the Fear of consequences.

So you are a Slave to the one who sends out Curses. YES, THE Shadow.

But remember the Shadow has no servants to do Its will when you speak Truth. Yes, No-One can or will dispute Reality. One only disputes Lies and Illusions, and becomes a Servant or Slave for the Shadow. But when you speak Truth you become a Servant and Master of your God and receive the REWARDS.

Yes, One is Leading you from Far out front by encouragement and a promise.

The Other is Pushing you from behind by Fear tactic and a threat.

One is Good, The Other is Waste.

oooooOooooo

oooooOooooo

"Saint Bill" says to the Human Race, "WE" are One. Not "I" am It. (Yes, God (The Spirit of Goodness) reaches out to All of Us, Unconditionally)

oooooOooooo

1) The Shadow says, I am God, Follow me and I will take you to Heaven. But It is a Liar, So It takes you to Hell the Long way around.

2) The Shadow says, I am God, If you do not follow me, you will go to Hell. But It is a Liar. God does not Curse or Threaten. God gave us a Free Will, So we can Follow what we please and we still go to Heaven because heaven is a Pre-Determined place; But God says, Use your Sense of Judgement and Sense of Reason and you will find Heaven on Earth.

The Shadow says, Do not Judge, so you fall into Pitfall after Pitfall.

oooooOooooo

"The COMPASS" is a Story of the Fight between the Good Guy and the Bad Guy., And the Good Guy wins Everytime, "Hands Down"., because the Good Guy is a mountain of a Spirit. The Bad Guy is a twisted Molehill.

oooooOooooo

oooooOooooo

God (The Spirit of Goodness) is never Con-fronted. It is always Far Far outfront Looking to the Future, and Never looks Back. Therefore God never Con-fronts Us, But rather always gives Us a Free Choice and Time to think so that we will come to Understand the Truth without Con-frontation and the unnecessary Pain that would follow.

But we are not God, and so we sometimes Con-front one-another because we think we are running out of Time. But we are Not running out of Time.

That is <u>another Illusion. Another Shadow.</u>

<u>(We are All Going to Heaven)</u>

The Tradition Of "Change For The Better"
Is Born In
P R E V I E W I S M

oooooOooooo

"YES"
So It is Written
So Shall It BE

oooooOooooo

PREVIEWS INC.

presents

Philosophy: PREVIEWISM

Founder: W.J. (Bill) Handel, M.A., L.W.

The Member: PREVIEWLITE

Place of Worship A SUMMIT

Worship Co-ordinator:

Phone: (403) 273-9182

For Orders or Inquiries:

PREVIEWS Inc.
4209 - 26th Avenue S.E.
Calgary, Alberta, Canada
T2B 0E1
Phone: (403) 273-9182

Price: $89.95   ISBN-0-9697487-0-1

HEAVEN
G O D
Truth

Reality

GOOD	**WHITE**	**LIGHT**
Blessings-Good	Lite Lite Grey	Knowledge Innocent
↑ One Way	Grey - Humanbeings	↑ One Way
Punishment-waste	Dark Dark Grey	Innocent Ignorance
BAD	**BLACK**	**Darkness**

Illusion

Lie

SHADOW

HELL

P R E V I E W S

" Institute of Universal Philosophy "

Non-Profit

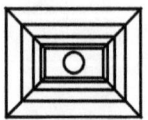

The Star
of
PREVIEWS

FOUNDED BY: "THE COMPASS"
Author: W. J. (BILL) HANDEL, M.A., L.W.
Alias: "SAINT BILL"

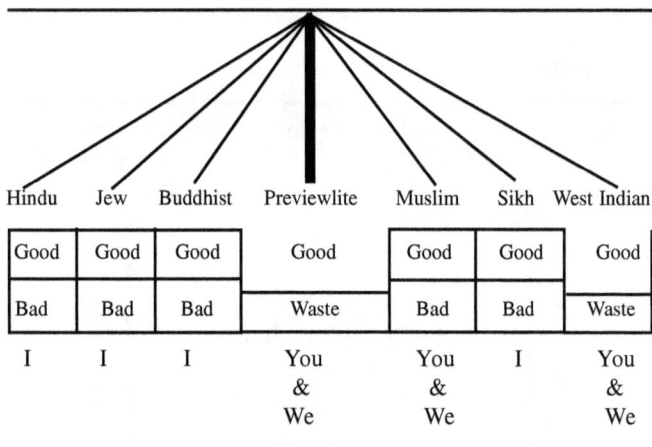

Hindu	Jew	Buddhist	Previewlite	Muslim	Sikh	West Indian
Good	Good	Good	Good	Good	Good	Good
Bad	Bad	Bad	Waste	Bad	Bad	Waste
I	I	I	You & We	You & We	I	You & We

are MultiCulturalist

Yes, God (the Real) is a MultiCulturalist; God (the Fraud) is a Separatist.

We	I
are	am
One	It

Previewlites are by Nature Canadian and Canadians believe in MultiCulturalism. An old Proverb says, "When you are in rome, do as the Romans do." Well, all you "I"'s, you are in Canada now and you are welcome but if you can not stand the Heat get out of the Kitchen. The Immigration doors are open.

"Good" Direction Is Our Business: You May Call Us Now!!
4209 - 26th Avenue S.E., Calgary, Alberta T2B 0E1 • Phone {403} 273-9182
THE TRADITION OF " CHANGE FOR THE BETTER"
IS BORN IN
P R E V I E W I S M

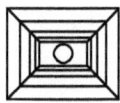

PREVIEWISM
Our World is Beautiful, Yes, Multi-Cultural

The Foundation of any True Religion is that God created Humankind in Its Image with a "Good" nature; and this once done is forever done because God is Unconditionally Loving and Unconditionally Forgiving and does not Condemn.

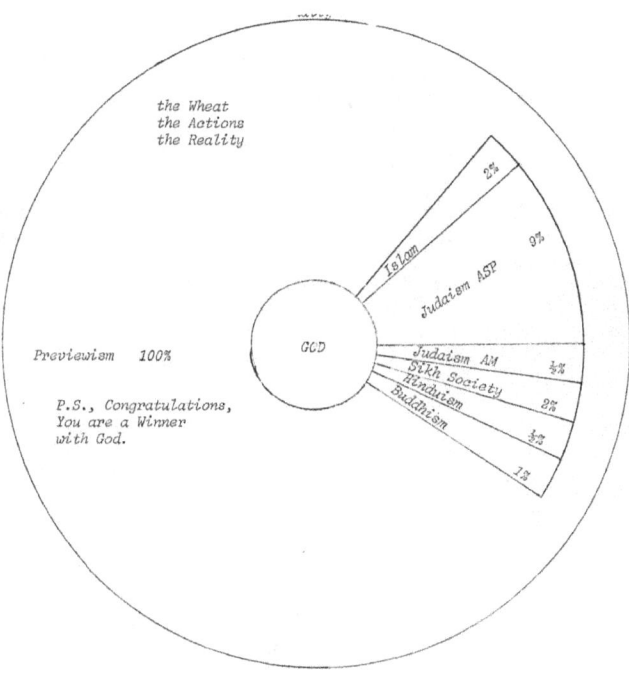

The above Graph is with respect to the Canadian populace.

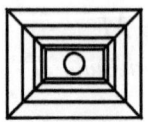

P R E V I E W S

" Institute of Universal Philosophy "

Non-Profit

The Star
of
PREVIEWS

FOUNDED BY: "THE COMPASS"
Author: W. J. (BILL) HANDEL, M.A., L.W.
Alias: "SAINT BILL"

*ooooo*O*ooooo*

CERTIFICATE OF MEMBERSHIP
for
_____

This is to Certify that the above named was Elected a member in Good Standing of "Preview Institute of Universal Philosophy" on _____ and is entitled to all the Privileges of such Membership and Furthermore is hereby Encouraged to Advance the OBJECTS of our Charter, being:

1) To make and keep people Happy go Lucky. 2) to keep people Free of Guilt, Fear, Doubt and illusion. 3) To set in people a frame of Mind to achieve the above. 4) To bring people to live in Harmony with one another. 5) to bring people to leave this world a better place than when they came into it. 6) To distribute the wealth and abundance of Gods' food and Essentials of life to the Needy throughout the world. 7) To bring "The Gospel of Saint BILL", that being "The Free Spirit of god", "The Spirit of Truth", Yes, "The Spirt of Goodness" as manifested in and by "The Compass" to the World at large and to organize, co-ordinate and direct the Energies of Its' 5.1 Billion members in the same direction at the same time, for a Loving force to be reckoned with, to the Glory of God. 8) To bring "Heaven to Earth" so that we might enjoy a little of Heaven while we are here on Earth. 9) To Foster and Develop among Its members and the world at large, a recognition of the importance of the "Good Natured God" in their life and for they themselves to Foster and Develop their "Good Nature" as a compliment to Our Dear God. 10) To establish and maintain buildings for worship and other religious use. 11) to organize and provide religious instruction, and to perform pastoral work. 12) To place a copy of "The COMPASS" in every Home in every Country of the World, as soon as possible, by Sale and/or by Gift. In Summary, #13) To Relieve Poverty. (Both Physical and Spiritual poverty)

President	$\overline{M}$ $\overline{D}$ $\overline{YR}$	Secretary-Treasurer
W.J. (Bill) Handel, M.A., L.W.,	*ooooo*O*ooooo*	Nafisa Walji

"Good" Direction Is Our Business: You May Call Us Now!!
4209 - 26th Avenue S.E., Calgary, Alberta T2B 0E1 • Phone {403} 273-9182
THE TRADITION OF " CHANGE FOR THE BETTER"
IS BORN IN
P R E V I E W I S M

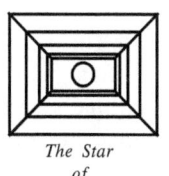

P R E V I E W S Inc

"Eternal (TRUST) Foundation"

The Star of PREVIEWS

FOUNDED BY: "THE COMPASS"
Author: "SAINT BILL"
Revealed By: "The Spirit of Truth"

The Charity Affiliate: "Previews Institute of Universal Philosophy" (NON-PROFIT)

Dear Friends,. Join our "One Book per Month" Club and be eligible to receive a Pension income beginning at age 60, between $480.00 to $1,008.00 per month C$ subject to your present age of course, and your closing ratio.

If you are between the age of 18 to the age of 40 you are eligible ot join the Club.. Club members purchase "One Book per Month" and give It away to a Friend or Aquaintance. For every one of these people who join the Club, the asponsoring Club member receives a 20% commision, which is held in trust by "Previews Inc." until the Sponsor is age 60. At this point you being to receive your Pension for the Life of you, as you continue to be a Club member.

We at "Previews" are confident we have a "Best Seller" inthe Philosophy as manfested in and by "The COMPASS". It is a truly positive and Happy-go-Lucky approach to life on Earth and in Heaven, as we know that God the Real, "The Spirit of Goodness" is always Everunderstanding, Loving, and Forgiving, and has no plans for you other than "Eternal Life in heaven with God".

If you are interested in further details in this regard, please do not hesitate to contact your Sponsoring Club member. You will find that there is no better investment than investing in the Advancement of All of Humankind in the Spiritual sense, because "Spiritual Success" leads to "Material Success". Yes, this is "The Relief of Poverty". Yes, "A Charity", and the Returns are Great!!

Thank you for your interest and we hope to hear from you soon,
Yours truly, as ever in, "The Spirit of Goodness",

Previews Inc. (Eternal "Trust" Foundation)

Per: Wilhelm J. (Bill) Handel, M.A., L.W., (Executor)

(YOU will be Interested in Becoming a "FOUNDING PARTNER", when you Understand our Object) "Call or Come in, Now!!!!"

"Specializing in "Food for THOUGHT"
Since 1990 (51 B.H.)
4209 - 26th Avenue S.E., Calgary, Alberta T2B 0E1
THE TRADITION OF "CHANGE FOR THE BETTER"
IS BORN IN
P R E V I E W I S M

Dear Friends and Children of All ages: There are Three segments of people in Society. Two are Wrong, One is Right. Most of Society is in their Right frame of Mind most of the time. Some of Society are in their Right frame of Mind all of the time. Some of Society are in the Wrong frame on Mind all the time. It is those that provide us with the Biggest Challenge.

Yes, we must not give-up on the Insane, because they are just living in Illusion and at any time they may See or Hear something that will bring them to Reality. And we know that Reality is God and God is Reality, Not Fantasy.

Some people think that God wants a Sacrifice, that is Illusion. Some people think that Illusion can become a Reality, that is Illusion. Illusion is Illusion, and Reality is Reality. Some people Act on Illusion and cause pain and Suffering. Some people Act on Reality and cause Happiness, Decency, Prosperity and Peace of Mind. Yes, nothing but Blessings. Thank God for Reality.

We know that God is the same Yesterday, Today, and tomorrow, but at the same time Always making Progress and Improving Its Quality and quantity of Goodness, knowing that It will Ultimately reach Its Goal of Heaven on Earth,. Imperfect as God is, but none the less, Heaven on Earth.

Some people think that God can become a Person, that is Illusion. Some people think that Illusion can become a Person, that is Illusion upon Illusion. (Satan) Some people think that Satan lives in people, that is Illusion, Satan is Illusion and does not exist in any way, shape or form. It is just plain simple Illusion, Cast It Out. That is Right, Cast It Out of your Mind and let Reality which is God live in your Heart, Mind, and Soul. This brings you All the Blessings of God the Real, "The Spirit of Goodness", and all of Its children (angels), the Oldest being "The Spirit of Truth" and the Youngest being "The Spirit of Enthusiasm". All of God's children have a "Sense of Judgement", a "Free Spirit", and a "Good Nature". Let them Flourish and God will be Glorified.

Once upon a time a certain group of people Killed a man because they thought he was Satan. After they Killed him, they came to Realize that he was Just A Man. And so to overcome their Shame they said they seen him Rise from the Dead and ultimately float up into the Clouds. They realized he had been serving god, so they said He was God on Earth, but gone to heaven. Poor people, they further tried to Justify Murder by saying that god wanted a Sacrifice and that they had Served God. But they knew that God says, "Thou Shalt not Kill", but their Shame was so Great that they preferred to Justify Murder, and continued to preach their Lies and Illusions. Yes, the Lies and Illusions of the Dark ages.

Yes, folks, these people did not realize that God does not want a Sacrifice but that God wants Obedience to Its Good words. And that when God does not get Obedience, It says, Forgiven,. "Go, and do it better next time, now that you have learned Reality from Illusion". But this group of people has not learn a thing, because they would do the same thing over again if someone confronted them with The Reality of God as "The Spirit of Goodness", and not the Illusion of Self-righteousness, Extortion, and Self-servance, and Perfection. Insanity.

Dear Friends, we think you got the Picture, so we will leave it at that.

Thanks for Listening, as ever in, "The Spirit of Goodness",
W.J. (Bill) Handel, M.A., L.W.
alias "Saint Bill" (Head Coach)
Previews Institute, "Summit Loc- 001, H.0."

1/3

Dear Friends: "Saint Jesus" together with "Saint Bill" and a whole host of other "Saints", represent God the Real, "The Spirit of Goodness", and not God the Fraud, "Illusion". Yes, today we are going to draw you a Picture. (Acts 26, vs. 16-18 (John 7, vs.16-18) (1 Jn. 4, v.20) (2 Thes. 2, v.9-11)

In the Beginning there were three (3) entities. The first was God, the second was "The Messiah" and the third was "Adam and Eve". Yes, Adam and Eve are One, So there were three Entities.

God had a conversation with "Adam and Eve" first. Yes, God said, to Its Children, I want you to know that "Life is Eternal". Yes, we have "Life in the Womb" "Life on Earth", and "Life in heaven", and each is Eternal unto Its own and are One as we recycle into and out of "The Future".

Now, I want to ask you a question, Children,. "Do you want to be a Slave, or do you want to be Free?,. And Adam and Eve said, "We want to be FREE!!!".

And God said, "Go, You are FREE".

Then "The Messiah" said, Wait, You must not use your "Sense of Judgement", Yes, Do not Judge, Do not Decide right from wrong, or you will Die.

Then God said , "You are a Liar",. Stay out of My Sight.. You illegit.

Then Adam and Eve asked, "Who should we Believe?", and God said, "You are Free", "Take your Choice"..... Then Adam and Eve decided to Eat.. and God said, God Bless you, Children, God Bless you!!

Yes, folks, most of us Use our"Sense of Judgement" to Judge (Decide) right from wrong, and make progress in Happiness, Decency, Prosperity, and Peace of Mind. And know without a doubt that "Life is Eternal", knowing that Physical Death is just an Illusion trying to distract us from the Reality of Life Eternal

A few of us are misled by Illusion (The Shadow), the Fear monger, Extortionist, Self-server, and Perfectionist,. and Live in Misery. But all is not lost because we are all God's children and God Forgives us our shortcomings and allows "Life Eternal" to continue,. Heaven on Earth without End.

Thank you, Dear God, Thank you.
Trusting you got It, we remain, as ever in,
"The Spirit of Goodness",.
"Saint Bill".

WE

are Created, Conceived, and Born in the Image of God. We are Young and Ignorant while God is Old and Wise. We have much to Learn. But, We are considered Equal and One with God, and God is considered Equal and One with Us, always. God the Real, "The Spirit of Goodness", with Its "Sense of Judgement, "Free Spirit", and "Good Nature", together with Its children (angels), the Oldest being "The Spirit of Truth" and the Youngest being "The Spirit of Enthusiasm", with many in between, Lives in heaven, in the World, and in our Heart, Mind, and Soul. It never Dies, but Recycles into and out of the Future when our Bodies cease to function, and when we are Created.

WE

are FORGIVEN before we start our Day, and we are FORGIVEN after we end our Day, and while we Sleep we can do Nothing wrong. So we are always
Saints.

WE

are IMMORTAL, Yes, once Created there is no looking back. Yes, Life in the Womb, Life on Earth, and Life in Heaven.. GUARANTEED in writing by "The COMPASS", by Author: "Saint Bill", A Servant for God's sake, (The Roots, Acts 26, v. 16-18) (John 7, v.16-18) (1 Jn.4, v.20) (2 Thes.2, v.9-11) (The Seed, Instinctive Genius). (The Tree, Love and forgiveness) (The Fruit, Happiness, Decency, Prosperity, and

Peace of Mind.

Thanks again for Listening, as ever in,
"The Spirit of Goodness
B.H., M.A., L.W. "Saint Bill" (Head Coach)
Previews Institute of Universal Philosophy
"Summit Loc-001, H.O)."

OVERLAP TO "OBJECT, MASTERS DEGREE"

Dear Friends and Children of All ages: The Reality of Life is that It is Eternal in Body, Mind, and Spirit. Yes, Into and Out of the Future, world without End. Yes, the Circle (Cycle) of Life is very Large, so Large that we think we are travelling in a Straight Line, but It is a Long Curve that forms a Circle, and so It is Never Ending.

When we are Conceived, the Spirit becomes Body (Life in the Womb), then the Body becomes Word (Life on Earth), then the Word becomes Spirit (Life in heaven). Yes, from Beginning to Present, and from Present to beginning, and from beginning to Beginning, and from Beginning to Present, and so on and on, World without End.

The Complete Cycle spans approximately 300 years from Birth to Re-Conception. That is approximately 100 years on Earth (seldom over 111), and approximately 200 years in Heaven (seldom over 222), then It is back to Body. This spells "Eternal Life", and a Life of Bliss,. All else is a story of The Shadow, pure Bad Fiction (Illusion). Yes, there is No longer any Curse. (Rev. 22, v.3)

And so you See, Folks, the World is a Beautiful place to Live in,. But The Shadow (Illusion) (Satan) says, The World is Bad,. And Its Institution is Good. But we know that Satan (The Shadow) is a Liar. Its Institution is trying to Rule the world by using "Fear Tactic", and NEGATIVE, Sadistic, Mean, Lazy, Shameless, Self-righteous, Extortionist, Parasitic psychology called "Sadism".

But God will not allow it, because God has given the World a "Sense of Judgement", a "Free Spirit", and a "Good Nature", and many POSITIVE characteristics (angels), the oldest being The Spirit of Truth, and the youngest being The Spirit of Enthusiasm, with many in between that results in "Happyism", and this keeps the Unfullfilling Influence of The Shadow (Satan) (Illusion) under control and reduced to Less than a Speck of Dust, for 88% of the World's population.

So you see, God rules the World, and the Self-righteous idiots can Lie all they want, and gain nothing but Pain and Suffering for themselves,. Yes, The Shadow Worshippers.

But, God being in control, Forgives even The Shadow Worshippers, and allows Life to continue, Heaven on Earth, World without End.

Oh, Yes, We have herein a "New Psychology" according to "The Spirit of Goodness", God the Real, as manifested in and by "The Compass", a New Bible, The EverLast Testament, by Author: "Saint Bill", and in 300 years We will be back to enjoy the Fruits of my Labor........Chuckle, Chuckle, eh!!

Thank you, Dear God, Thank you, for true Insight.
Thank you, Dear God, Thank you, "We are All Saints" in God's eye, and We Look at Life through God's eye..

Thanks for Listening, Folks, It was a Pleasure,
As ever in, "The Spirit of Goodness",
"Saint Bill", A Servant for God's sake.

Note: 88% of people are Positive, and to some degree negative.
 12% of people are Negative, and to some degree positive.
And the Majority Rules among the Wise.
(Yes, a Democracy works Best)

"SPECIAL"

LIFE-TIME
MEMBERSHIP
for

_____

with
PREVIEWS
"Institute of Universal Philosophy"
_____

Assuming YOU Accept THREE "COMPASS"
For the Price of "TWO"

That is Right, this "COMPASS" is given to you for "FREE" with the Assumption that you will Buy "TWO" every Three months, to give to your New found Friends for "FREE", with the same Assumption, for the Life-of-your Membership.

      Thank you, DEAR God, Thank you

SPONSOR _____

        S#_____

Dated:_____A.B.

5,939 A.M
       "Let Us keep in Touch"

     Phone: _____

www.ingramcontent.com/pod-product-compliance
Lightning Source LLC
Chambersburg PA
CBHW071300110426
42743CB00042B/1123